fundamentals of venture capital

Fundamentals of

Venture Capital

Joseph W. Bartlett

MADISON BOOKS
Lanham • New York • Oxford

Published by Madison Books
4720 Boston Way
Lanham, Maryland 20706

12 Hid's Copse Road
Cumnor Hill, Oxford OX2 9JJ, England

Distributed by National Book Network

Library of Congress Cataloging-in-Publication Data

Bartlett, Joseph W., 1933– .
    Fundamentals of venture capital / Joseph W. Bartlett.
      p. cm.
    Includes bibliographical references and index.
    ISBN 1-56833-126-6 (alk. paper)
    1. Venture capital.
  HG4751.B36   1999
  658.15′224—dc21

                              99-047550

contents

chapter eight

You've Set up the Company and Negotiated the Price:
What Are the Investors' Terms?   79

chapter nine

I Have a Letter of Intent: What's in the Contract?   98

chapter ten

Selling Stock, Privately . . . and Legally   108

chapter eleven

Compensating Your Key Executives

chapter twelve

How to Go to the Promised Land (i.e., Go Public)

chapter thirteen

Financing with Strategic Investors: Joint Ventures

Conclusion

chapter one

What Is All the Talk About?

Confounding many of its critics of a few years ago, the American economy is outstripping the economies of its sister industrial nations by an astonishing margin. The United States has been breathtakingly successful in creating new jobs. While Europeans are experiencing double-digit unemployment, the U.S. economic engine continues to roar, combining low unemployment and low inflation in ways which seem to puncture the accepted econometric models. The Japanese miracle, the Pacific Rim tigers . . . little need be said about their recent fall from grace, except that it has happened despite educated workforces, positive balances of payments, high savings rates, strong productivity, and a work ethic which equals if not exceeds that prevalent in the United States. What is going on here? We are not the richest nation in terms of natural resources (although, of course, we are blessed); Russia certainly has more of everything the world needs to run its factories. We run a balance-of-payments deficit year in and year out and, until recently, a deficit in our own internal accounts. Other indices, infant mortality, for example, and secondary education are not wholly favorable. What constitutes the critical distinction?

I suggest that a major, although not the only, difference between the U.S. economy and those of the other nation states with which we compare ourselves lies in a confluence of happy factors, some created by design and some serendipitous, which came together after World War II, under the heading of "Venture Capital." Entrepreneurs, investors, scientists, and key managers have coalesced in various hot spots around this country over the past forty years to incubate new firms, most but not certainly all technologically oriented, which have grown from classic garage start-ups to multibillion-dollar corporations such as Microsoft, Intel, Compaq, and the like. Only in America, it seems, have the necessary constituent elements been successfully combined to create an economic powerhouse.

Under the loose heading of the term "Venture Capital," U.S. firms both large and small have fully appreciated the thesis that, in order to avoid the necessary stagnation predicted by neo-Marxist economists, business and industry must continually innovate. When foreign students enroll in my class at New York University Law School, they come to learn the process of innovation from someone who has been in the business for over thirty-five years. They are armed with the accepted and revealed wisdom that innovation is the key to both micro- and macro-economic success. Thus, statistical evidence indicates that new job creation over the past twenty years has been almost exclusively fomented by hiring at firms with fewer than a hundred employees. The jury, in a word, is no longer out. Venture capital is what makes the wheels turn in this country; the phenomenon appears to be, by and large, peculiar to this country, indeed peculiar to specific regions of the country. Other nations house some interesting venture-capital companies; the United Kingdom and Israel particularly come to mind. However, in my experience, sooner or later most of those firms come to the United States to do business—to learn, to obtain capital, to soak up the entrepreneurial spirit. The United States has no monopoly on science; but transforming that science into major commercial enterprises seems to be U.S.-specific.

The point, in short, is that the devil is in the details. Most economists and businessmen around the world understand the magic of venture capital. There are would-be entrepreneurs with unflagging spirits around the globe and interesting and distinguished science coming out of first-class universities and research centers. Government support and subsidy is available and the will to emulate the United States is palpable. The fact is, however, that doing venture capital is hard; it requires not only luck and pluck but also knowledge of the terrain and a keen appreciation for those particular items which have to go into the mix before a successfully backed firm is generated.

WHAT IS VENTURE CAPITAL?

The composer of the term "venture capital" is unknown, and there is no standard definition of it. It is, however, generally agreed that the traditional venture-capital era began in earnest in 1946, when General Georges Doriot, Ralph Flanders, Karl Compton, Merrill Griswold and others organized American Research & Development (AR&D), the first (and, after it went public, for many years the only) public corporation specializing in investing in illiquid securities of early stage issuers.

One way to define traditional "venture capital," therefore, is to repeat General Doriot's rules of investing, the thought being that an investment process entailing Doriot's rules is, by definition, a venture-capital process. According to Doriot, investments considered by AR&D involved: (1) new technology, new marketing concepts, and new product application possibilities; (2) a significant, although not necessarily controlling, participation by the investors in the company's management; (3) investment in ventures staffed by people of outstanding competence and integrity (herein the rule often referred to in venture capital as "bet the jockey, not the horse"); (4) products or processes which have passed through at least the early prototype stage and are adequately protected by patents, copyrights, or trade-secret agreements (the latter rule is often referred to as investing in situations where the information is "proprietary"); (5) situations which show promise to mature within a few years to the point of an initial public offering or a sale of the entire company (commonly referred to as the "exit strategy"); and (6) opportunities in which the venture capitalist can make a contribution beyond the capital dollars invested (often referred to as the "value-added strategy").

General Doriot's boundary conditions are to be treated with great deference because it is commonly agreed that Doriot is the single most significant figure in postwar traditional venture capital. Not only did he provide AR&D with its primary guidance (until it was acquired by Textron), but he also introduced a significant percentage of today's senior venture capitalists to the business through the courses he taught at Harvard Business School. And he showed the world how a traditional venture-capital investment strategy could produce enormous rewards when AR&D's modest investment in Digital Equipment Corporation (DEC) ballooned into investor values in the billions.

Parenthetically, in the eyes of the public of his day, Doriot's record at AR&D included only a few "home runs"—DEC in particular—and a bunch of losers, leading inexperienced observers to conclude that a well-managed venture portfolio should concentrate on the long ball, so to speak—the one investment that will return two or three hundred times one's money and justify a drab performance by the rest of the portfolio. This fallacious conclusion fostered the 1960s notion that an ultra–high-risk strategy is characteristic of venture-capital investing, with managers plunging exclusively into new and untried schemes with the hope of "winning big" every now and then. In fact, the AR&D strategy was never tied to the solo home run. Moreover, venture strategies have become highly varied. Some venture pools focus in whole or in part on late-round investments: infusions of cash shortly before the company is planning to go public, for example. Moreover, as outlined subsequently, buyouts involving mature firms are a popular venture strategy, as are so-called turnarounds, investments in troubled companies, including some actually in bankruptcy. And some funds are hybrids, sharing more than one strategy, even including a portion of the assets invested in public securities. The point is that a venture manager balances risk against reward; a "pre-seed" investment should forecast sensational returns, while a late-round purchase of convertible debt will promise a more modest payoff.

The term "venture capital" is grammatically multifaceted. General Doriot's exegesis specifies a certain type of investment as characteristic of the venture universe. He assumes, a priori, the proposition that venture capital involves a process, the making and managing (and ultimately selling) of investments. In addition, the phrase is sometimes used as an adjective applied to players in the game; that is, "venture-backed companies," meaning the portfolio opportunities in which the venture-capital partnerships or "funds" invest. The phrase becomes a noun when it describes the capital provided by individuals, families, and firms, which entities, along with the partnership managers, are called *venture capitalists*.

In terms of the people involved, venture capital is an intense business. The symbiotic relationship between the venture capitalist and his investment (assuming he is the "lead investor," meaning the investor most closely identified with the opportunity) is such that each professional can carry a portfolio of no more than a handful of companies. The investors are usually experienced professionals with formal academic training in business and finance and on-the-job training as apprentices at a venture fund or financial institution. Their universe is still relatively small; they and their advisers tend to be on a first-name basis, veterans of a deal or two together. And the work is hard, particularly since on-site visits impose an enormous travel burden.

The venture-capital process, before it was so labeled, has existed for centuries; antedating American Research & Development, it is as old as commercial society itself. In this century, for example, Vanderbilt interests financed Juan Trippe in the organization of Pan American Airways, Henry Ford was financed by Alexander Malcolmson, and Captain Eddie Rickenbacker was able to organize Eastern Airlines in the 1930s with backing from the Rockefellers. However, the era of professionally managed venture capital—pools of money contributed by unrelated investors and organized into separate legal entities, managed by experts according to stated objectives, set forth in a contract between managers and investors, describing a structured activity, an activity that conforms to definite (albeit changing) patterns and rules—is a process that dates from the organization of AR&D.

In sum, the term *venture capital* can be applied in a number of ways: to investments, people, or activities. With full appreciation for the multiple uses of the term, the thrust and emphasis of this book (although by no means exclusively) is on venture capital of the type which is compatible with the Doriot rules. First, venture capital is an activity involving the investment of funds. It ordinarily involves investments in illiquid securities, which carry higher degrees of risk (and commensurately higher possibilities of reward) than so-called traditional investments in the publicly traded securities of mature firms. The venture-capital investor ordinarily expects that his participation in the investment (or the participation of one of the investors in the group which he has joined, designated usually as the "lead investor") will add value, meaning that the investors will be able to provide advice and counsel designed to improve the chances of the investment's ultimate success. The investment is made with an extended time horizon, required by the fact that the securities are illiquid. (In this connection, most independent venture funds are partnerships scheduled to liquidate ten to twelve years from inception, in turn suggesting that a venture-capital investment is expected to become liquid somewhere around four to six years from initial investment.)

Since the most celebrated rewards in the past have generally accrued to investments involving advances in science and technology to exploit new markets, traditional venture-capital investment is often thought of as synonymous with high-tech start-ups. However, as stated earlier, that is not an accurate outer boundary, even in the start-up phase. For example, the technology of one of the great venture-capital winners—Federal Express—is as old as the Pony Express, and it would take a great stretch of the imagination to perceive of fast-food chains such as McDonald's as involving additions to our store of scientific learning. But, whether high or low tech, the traditional venture capitalist thrives when the companies in which he invests have an advantage over potential competition in a defined segment of the market, often referred to as a "niche." The product or service is as differentiated as possible, not a "commodity." Exploitation of scientific and technological breakdowns has, historically, been a principal way (but not the only way) for emerging companies to differentiate themselves from their more mature and better-financed competitors.

How Venture Capitalists Talk

The discussion in this book will make use of terminology commonly used in the venture world. First, the entities into which capital sources are aggregated for purposes of making investments are usually referred to as "funds," "venture companies," or "venture partnerships." They resemble mutual funds in a sense but are not, with rare exceptions (AR&D was one), registered under the Investment Company Act of 1940 because they are not publicly held and do not offer to redeem their shares frequently or at all. The paradigmatic venture fund is an outgrowth of the Greylock model, a partnership with a limited group of investors, or limited partners, and an even more limited group of managers who act as general partners, the managers enjoying a so-called carried interest, entitling them to a share in the profits of the partnership in ratios disproportionate to their capital contributions. Venture funds include federally assisted Small Business Investment Companies (which can be either corporations or partnerships) and, on occasion, a publicly held corporation along the AR&D model, styled since 1980 as "business development corporations." This book, following common usage, will refer to any managed pool of capital as a "fund" or "partnership."

Once a fund makes an investment in an operating entity, the fund or group of funds doing the investing are the "investors." A company newly organized to exploit an idea is usually called a "start up," founded by an individual sometimes referred to as the "entrepreneur" or the "founder." Any newly organized company, particularly in the context of a leveraged buyout (LBO), is routinely labeled "Newco." The stock issued by a founder to himself (and his key associates) is usually sold for nominal consideration and those shares are labeled "founders stock." (The use of the male gender is used throughout for ease of reference only.) The founder, as he pushes his concept, attracts professional management, usually known as the "key employees." If his concept holds particular promise he may seek from others (versus providing himself) the capital required to prove that the concept works—that is, the capital invested prior to the production of a working model or prototype. This is called "seed investment" and the tranche is called the "seed round." Each financing in the venture process is referred to as a "round" and given a name or number: "seed" round, "first venture" round, "second" round, "mezzanine" round, and so forth.

Once the prototype has been proven in the lab, the next task ordinarily is to place it in the hands of a customer for testing—called the "beta test" (the test coming after the lab, or "alpha," test). At a beta test site(s), the machine or process will be installed free and customers will use and debug it over a period of several weeks or months. While the product is being beta tested, capital is often raised to develop and implement a sales and marketing strategy, the financing required at this stage being, as indicated above, "the first venture round."

The next (and occasionally the last) round is a financing calculated to bring the company to cash break-even. Whenever a robust market exists for initial public offerings—for example, the late 1960s, 1983, 1986, 1993—this round is often financed by investors willing to pay a relatively high price for the security on the theory that their investment will soon be followed by a sale of the entire company or an initial public offering. Hence, this round is often called the "mezzanine round." A caution at this juncture: The term "mezzanine" has at least two meanings in venture-capital phraseology. It also appears as a label for junior debt in leveraged buyouts. In either event, it means something right next to or immediately anterior to something else. As used in venture finance, the financing is next to the occasion on which the founder and investors become liquid—an initial public offering (IPO) or sale of the entire company. As indicated earlier, the measures taken to get liquid are categorized as the "exit strategies."

One of the critical elements in venture investing is the rate at which a firm incurs expenses, since most financings occur at a time when the business has insufficient income to cover expenses. The monthly expense burden indicates how long the company can exist until the next financing, and that figure is colorfully known as the "burn rate." (Other common terms are defined as they appear in this book.)

SHOULD YOU START YOUR OWN COMPANY?

Prior to preparation of a business plan, the entrepreneur should ask some hard questions. Hundreds of thousands of new businesses are organized in the United States each year; unhappily, most of them fail within the first year or so. Since the great majority of start-ups are financed out of the pockets of their founders, the high failure rate should be a sobering statistic for would-be entrepreneurs. It may be fortunate for the economy as a whole that so few are daunted by the sober statistics, but it is hard on the individuals who do not make it. Nonetheless, available literature on the business aspects of organizing one's own firm rarely inquires into this threshold issue of whether one should set out on one's own in the first instance.

Much of the popular material on venture capital is potentially misleading in its ebullient optimism. It can be hard to keep one's head in the face of popular literature extolling the giant winners in the game—Jobs, Wozniak, Wang, and their peers, creators of new technologies which dominate the market and return hundreds of times the initial investment. The giants are an integral part of the mystique of venture capital, but an Apple Computer or Wang Laboratories comes along once in a lifetime. The odds against hitting that big are astronomical. Accordingly, books which record the anecdotal history of how Ken Olson organized Digital Equipment, how Ed DeCastro put together Data General, make fine reading, but the home-run expectations they promote can be dangerously intoxicating. A founder faced with the "go, no go" decision—whether or not to invest his entire savings in a new enterprise—is fooling himself if he stacks the reward side of the equation with the possibility of making hundreds of millions of dollars. It sometimes happens, of course, and someone has to win the lottery, but the vision of those sugarplums is not a sound basis for an intelligent investment decision. To be sure, it remains realistic for many founders to think of big rewards, perhaps even millions of dollars, albeit after a period of enormously hard work and great risk. Nonetheless, it is important to understand that in the vast majority of the cases—indeed, for the majority of the survivors—the returns on the founder's investment (and that investment must be calculated to include opportunity costs and sweat equity) are modest. Many founders find that, at the end of the game, they have either lost money or been working for a peon's wages.

There is a saying, attributed to Lord Palmerston, that many foolish wars have been started because political leaders got to reading small maps. Many businesses have been imprudently started because of the founder's inability to understand how difficult it is to achieve a double-digit compounded rate of return. Venture investments have, in fact, outperformed the stock market in the postwar years and, in many cases, quite handsomely. There have been periods when 25 percent compounded rates of return have been available to the investors; indeed, substantially higher rates have been achieved by many venture funds, and over long periods of time. But it is an economic impossibility to compound any substantial sum of money at a 25-percent rate of return indefinitely unless the investors are entitled to believe they will own all the assets in the world within one man's lifetime. It has been remarked that one of the greatest individual fortunes assembled in this country in recent years is that of J. Paul Getty, who started with a modest stake as a young man and wound up with a personal fortune in excess of $3 billion. It is a wildly successful story, but sobering when one considers that Getty's annual compounded rate of return on his initial few thousand dollars has been calculated at about 14 percent. In short, in reading the success stories reprinted in the popular books, the part to focus on is the hard work and risk involved. Enormous returns are contingent and should not be the foundation of the analytical planning process.

"YOU CAN MAKE IT. . . . WILL SOMEONE BUY IT?"

Another major source of error is a love affair between a founder and the technology he has developed in the lab. The number of new and interesting ideas brought into being every year is astonishing. A field trip to any respectable college or university will reveal a fascinating array of projects in the laboratories, many of which, if brought to fruition, will certainly improve the state of the art. However, a critical error of founders considering whether to commit capital to a project is to assume that the novelty and utility of a new technology are both necessary *and* sufficient for the success of a start-up. Novelty may be enough to secure a patent, but it is only one part of the venture-capital equation.

No one can make any money unless there is a market for the product, unless people are willing to buy it at a price that returns a profit to the manufacturer. Assuming the idea is any good, is there a market for it? This simple, banal truth is overlooked time and again by the fledgling entrepreneurs. Is there a market which can be penetrated at a reasonable cost? The classic example is the pen that writes under water—interesting technically but, as it turned out, no one wanted to buy one because no one wanted to write a letter beneath the waves. Thus, the single most commonly cited reason for failure of a start-up is the inability to implement a well-thought-out marketing plan. Selling is a matter of airplanes, hotel rooms, and shoe leather; as Willy Loman put it, "on the road with a smile and a shoe shine." Marketing, on the other hand, has to do with understanding the demand for the product, pricing strategy, evaluating channels of distribution, and maximizing dollars spent on sales. Moreover, the market has to be large enough to support an interesting company. The enterprise with less than $10 million in sales and nowhere to go is usually not a suitable target for venture-capital financiers. Companies of that size are known as the "walking dead" in a venture portfolio—too small to go public and too large to abandon.

chapter two

Where Should I Look for Seed Capital?

INTRODUCTION

Assuming a founder is content that his product is technically feasible and marketable, the chore of raising money—hiring capital—is paramount. The founder's problem is twofold: whether money can be raised at all, and, if so, at a cost which leaves something in the deal for the founder. The sources of investment capital are numerous, ranging from commercial banks making fixed-rate, secured loans to individual investors (so-called angels) willing to provide risk-equity capital in hopes of a spectacular return down the road. A number of guidebooks list the types of capital sources a founder may use, and others specify the name, address, and telephone number of particular firms. The discussion in this chapter will concern the potential sources, the legal constraints, and some of the problems and opportunities involved in hiring capital for an emerging company.

ANGELS

Sometimes, if the forecasted returns are not attractive to professionally managed venture funds, the founder can search for those rich individuals who are anxious to invest in start-ups, are not jaded like the "vulture capitalists," and will accept situations the professionals are unlikely to favor. The minimum investment required to join a private-venture pool is usually quite high—in seven figures—and many of the older pools are closed to outsiders. Public vehicles for venture investing are not common. Accordingly, individual-venture investors exist. The founder's task is to find them, through a combination of persistence and luck.

Angel investing has become more organized and significant as many of the professionally managed venture pools are increasingly less interested in the seed round. Most angel investing is a product of chance encounters or family and social relationships, a high net-worth individual exposed to an opportunity to invest because he happened to meet the entrepreneur at a social function or was drawn to the investment through word of mouth. The typical angel round involves an investment of $500,000 to a group of one to five individuals and is sometimes called the "Rolodex round" because the investors are names on the entrepreneur's rolodex. Angel investing has become somewhat more organized, as groups of high net-worth individuals with common investment goals have coalesced into, for example, the Band of Angels, a Silicon Valley organization, and the angel breakfast for participants sponsored by the New York New Media Association. The organized groups of Angels usually avoid publicity so as not to be inundated with applications. How do you find them? Word of mouth (networking at the local venture-capital club) or by fletcherizing the trade press, namely, the *Venture Capital Journal*, *The Private Equity Analyst*, and *Red Herring*.

SEED CAPITAL FROM VCs

The initial temptation to the impecunious entrepreneur is to circulate a business plan and funding proposal to all the neighboring firms listed in *Pratt's Guide*. However, that exercise is almost always futile. The so-called over-the-transom submissions are rarely if ever favored by professional managers, the hit rate being in the neighborhood of one in a thousand. The VCs either initiate their own projects, often finding a talented entrepreneur who has succeeded in bringing a start-up to fruition and backing him on whatever project he selects, or accepting specific recommendations from, say, a member of the

VC's scientific advisory board. Moreover, recent research discloses that much of the professionally managed "venture capital" is actually so-called mezzanine capital, meaning it is available only to those firms which have achieved at least adolescence, often defined as cash-flow break-even. On occasion, VCs will pop up at a specific event, say, one sponsored by a prominent investment bank, and look over the menu of the companies presenting; but it is difficult for an otherwise unconnected entrepreneur to make the venture-capital community come to them at the seed and founder's round stage. Usually, one or more rounds of angel investing is required so that the product and business has progressed to the point where a first professional or venture round is in order. At that stage, which usually implies not only proof of concept but significant cash flows and perhaps even cash-flow break-even, the word is out among the cognoscenti that the VCs are wont to come to the entrepreneur rather than vice versa—the mountain coming to Mohammed in other words.

On the other hand, if professional investors can be rounded up, their very presence in the deal can be beneficial. Thus, the intelligent founder will select (and sell his hardest to) those investors who are likely to add something to the offering other than, and in addition to, cash. Some investors have such prestige in the venture world that their election to invest in the first instance will attract additional capital, both in the round in which they participate and in later rounds. It is a wise issuer who carefully selects his partners—that is, investors from the pools such as Greylock, Bessemer, J. H. Whitney, Venrock, Sutter Hill, Mayfield, Brentwood, Kleiner Perkins. They and others are examples of venture funds with such reputations for sagacity that their existence in the buying group enhances the success of the offering. As any veteran of venture-capital financing can testify, the first question asked by a potential investor is "who else is in?"

Moreover, some venture funds are set up to add technical expertise in specific areas. For instance, Market Corporation of America's venture-capital affiliate, Marketcorp Venture Associates, has the opportunity to borrow the marketing expertise of the parent. The Yankee Group's consulting prowess in computer and telecommunications is available to the investments made by its affiliate, Battery Ventures. Bain Capital, an offshoot of Bain & Company, has access to one of the world's most prestigious consulting firms. A venture pool affiliated with a large bank-holding company holds out the possibility of a preferred relationship with the bank, although the problems inherent in being both a lender and an investor have generally inhibited, and rightly so, the bank-lending side from being intimately involved with the bank-venture investing side. And, a corporate ven-

ture partner brings to the table all the possibilities entailed in the cor-
porate-partnering relationship.

True start-up money is hard to find. To cite an example: A group
of asset managers broke out of Alex Brown, one of the leading investment banks in the venture-capital business, to raise a fund for early-
stage investment. They elected to site the fund in Boston, which
seemed to be Coals to Newcastle, since the early-stage investment
business started in Boston. The fact is, however, that many of the
venerable Boston firms which cut their teeth on some of the most celebrated venture-capital enterprises (Wang Laboratories, Digital Equipment, Prime, Data General) have exited the early-stage business and
are exclusively confining themselves to more conservative, later-stage
investments; hence, the idea of domiciling an early-stage fund in the
cradle of later stage funds.

STATE AID

The states are trying a number of devices to incubate technologically
oriented industry. The bottom line is a multitude of programs offering
"hard" inducements, for example, loans and investments from a state-
affiliated fund, plus "soft" dollars in the form of low-cost facilities and
services, and "backdoor" financing in the form of state tax deductions
and credits. Such programs are usually administered in conjunction
with a local college or university. A state agency will put up a modest
amount of actual cash for grants and/or equity and debt investment
and then sweeten the pot with such benefits as government procure-
ment set-asides; technical assistance; state tax credits; and "incubator"
space, meaning subsidized, low-cost laboratory and office space rein-
forced with tenant amenities, such as computer access, telephone
answering, conference facilities, and word processing.

In conjunction with direct assistance, several states attempt to
"pump prime" by establishing focused research centers. These are
established by fiat on campus, each center representing a consortium
of universities, private firms, and area economic-development organ-
izations, usually organized around a specific scientific discipline.
Whether such centers will actually give birth to a significant quantum of research which would not otherwise have found its way into
the open air remains unclear.

Programs such as these are available, to varying degrees, in almost
every state. However, the financial impact of the programs is not of
the make-or-break variety. Moreover, once having accepted government assistance, a firm is subject to conditions both special (i.e., locate
in a given area, hire local residents) and general (e.g., affirmative

action, union wages). If management finds it wants to move the plant to Taiwan to stay competitive, it may not be free to do so because of restrictions in loan agreements, which may survive even after the loan is repaid. Nonetheless, despite the popular joke (Q: "Name one of the three biggest lies in the world." A: "I'm from the government and I'm here to help you"), the advantages of government-sponsored assistance should not be sneezed at. Once a loan has been made, for example, the risks of a bureaucrat pulling the plug are not as formidable as in the private sector, since loss ratios are not an index of great significance in a public agency. An interesting anomaly in government-loan administration is that the proceeds from repayment are ordinarily credited to the general treasury rather than to the accounts of the agency concerned. Consequently, the people in charge are often indifferent to the issue of repayment, since the money is not "theirs."

FEDERAL GRANTS AND LOANS

The most significant program of federal government assistance to small business is the loan and loan guarantee program run since 1953 by the Small Business Administration (SBA), coupled in 1958 with the creation of privately owned concerns called Small Business Investment Companies (SBICs), which utilize funds obtained from the federal government at soft rates to finance small business. Both programs are administered by the SBA but have different impacts on early-stage financings.

An SBA loan (whether in the form of a direct loan from the SBA, or, more commonly, a bank loan guaranteed by the SBA) is, despite the favorable terms, the equivalent of bank financing. Although interest rates can be soft, a loan entails a promise of repayment within a finite period of time and an interest cost from the date the loan is made. Further, it introduces a partner to the enterprise with a lender's mentality. In the typical case, a guaranteed bank loan, the fact that the SBA guarantees 90 percent (or less) of the loan should give no encouragement that the bank is likely to relax its attitude toward repayment. A 90-percent guarantee is not a 100-percent guarantee; a commercial bank that routinely loses 10 percent of the principal of the loans it makes would soon be out of business. The 10-percent exposure is taken very seriously by the administering bank, and its officers can be expected to work hard to make sure it will be repaid. Moreover, the SBA ordinarily requires the founder(s) to guarantee loans personally, and on occasion its collection efforts are rigorous. If a $150,000 loan is secured by a second mortgage on the founder's home and all of his personal assets, there is always the question whether the government assistance is worth it in the first place. (Most banks are not set up to make SBA-guaranteed loans because of the red tape involved; most of the relatively small number that do have been designated by the SBA as "small business lending companies," meaning that processing time has been shortened.) The principal advantage of an SBA guaranteed loan is that the bank is likely to go higher in the loan-to-value ratio on tangible assets and to extend maturities. Much of the financing for franchises in recent years has been arranged with the benefit of SBA guarantees.

Small Business Investment Companies (SBICs) are privately organized corporations (or partnerships) licensed and regulated by the SBA. They are entitled to obtain leverage from the SBA, but, until recently, SBICs obtaining funds from the SBA had only one choice—to pay interest, albeit at favorable rates, meaning that an interest element is usually included in the investment made in each portfolio company. Compelled to achieve a return, SBICs had been, accordingly, typical late-round investors, advancing loans coupled with equity options, often subordinated convertible debt. That situation has now changed with the preferred securities program, which entails the licensing and funding of private equity pools sponsored by experienced VCs. The government's capital is in the form of preferred equity versus debt and matches private funding on a 2- or 3-to-1 basis. The regulatory constraints can be a nuisance but the program has been a success, although more for small buyouts than emerging growth companies, however.

The principal source of the federal-grants mechanism for start-up companies originated in 1982 with the Small Business Innovation Development Act, which inaugurated the Small Business Innovation Research Program (usually abbreviated as SBIR). SBIR grants range from $50,000 to $500,000 and a number of government agencies, including particularly the Department of Defense, participate in awarding grants to firms with fewer than five hundred employees. Start-ups in and around Rockville, Maryland, where the National Institutes of Health are located, and in and around northern Virginia, where ex-Department of Defense technicians tend to spin off, are known occasionally as the "Beltway Bandits" and are often first in line for SBIR grants.

COMMERCIAL BANKS

The question whether a start-up should rely on commercial bank financing (if obtainable) is to be approached quite cautiously. A commercial bank can make a very poor partner for a fledgling enterprise; the lenders tend to want their money back at just the wrong moment. Often the only type of bank financing available to a start-up is a

demand note secured by a floating lien on all the assets of the operation and the personal signature of the founder, a dangerous weapon
in the hands of a nervous bank. Moreover, bank lending to early-stage,
high-tech companies is on occasion the result of a fashionable wave in
banking circles, the thought being that banks should get in on the
"new" game by incubating clones of Wang Laboratories through judi-
cious extensions of credit to deserving entrepreneurs. The first problem is that only a limited number of commercial banks are staffed
with loan officers with the necessary experience to discriminate
among applicants in an area of lending where standard rules of thumb
and guidelines are out the window. (There are, of course, significant
exceptions.) Moreover, as fashions come, so fashions go. Long-time
players in the venture-capital game can cite a number of unfortunate
instances when senior bank officers, focusing on a well-publicized disaster in the high-tech business generally, have given the generic order
to the lending division to "tighten the screws." The problem, of
course, is that start-ups are very fragile animals; the slightest hiccup in
a bank, or any relationship, can strangle the baby in its crib, so to
speak. Even more tragic are instances where the bank becomes nervous about the loan in the early stages of a start-up's career, when earnings are following the well-known "hockey stick" path (i.e., trending
downward for a number of periods, usually at least one full year longer
than the projections suggest, followed by a sharp "ramp up" once the
company breaks through). The bank's anxiety having been excited by
the long slide downward, it springs the trap by cutting off credit and
marshaling assets at the very point when the company's good news is
just beginning. There are, to be sure, banks and there are *banks*. Some
banks, particularly those located in the classic high-tech areas, have
become experienced in lending to early-stage companies and are less
likely to panic. Indeed, some banks are willing to negotiate compensation for their added risk by accepting equity in the borrower—an
equity "kicker"—or an interest rate tied to a fixed base or index plus
increases, depending on the fortunes of the borrower.

SHOULD I HAVE A PLACEMENT AGENT?

Founders desperate for financing debate whether the faucet will turn
on if they engage a placement agent, a question to be addressed in a
real-world context. In the first place, the great majority of first-round
financings are not economically interesting to an investment banking
firm. The fee for a placement is usually in the range of 2 to 5 percent
of the amount raised. Assuming a $1 million first-round financing, a
fee of $20,000 to $50,000 is not likely to attract many takers in the

investment-banking fraternity, when fees for acting as financial adviser in contested merger-and-acquisition transactions run into eight figures. There are exceptions to this, as to any other proposition. Encore Computer, because of the splendid reputation of its founders, attracted a high degree of interest from major-bracket investment bankers in the seed round; William Poduska, on leaving Apollo Computer and organizing Stellar, was able to titillate investment-banking appetites to a fever pitch. (Neither firm, it should be noted, remains as an independent entity.) However, the traditional founder is wasting his time beating down the doors of the elite investment bankers to help him raise money in the early rounds. Smaller investment-banking houses, their sights set lower than Morgan Stanley or Goldman Sachs, are more likely candidates, but even they are not enthusiastic about hitting the pavement to arrange a first-round investment because the amount of work is enormous and the payoff is often chancy.

If an agent is engaged to place securities privately, he will surely act only on a best-efforts basis. A firm commitment in the early stages of a company's history, indeed a firm commitment on a private placement of any kind, is encountered only in special circumstances. Moreover, the founder should understand that the agent is not obligated to sell an untried security; that remains the responsibility of the founder. The agent is engaged to help prepare a private placement memorandum and to expose the opportunity to a list of prospects, to screen buyers, and to schedule meetings for the founder to do his stuff. Purchasers in early rounds are not interested in discussing the merits of the investment with a salesman. The founder, and only the founder, has that reservoir of knowledge about the technology and its potential application which potential buyers are interested to hear. Moreover, the agent will look to the founder for a so-called friends list—that is, potential investors already known to the founder.

More importantly, the placement agent will usually insist on a right, in the nature of a first-refusal right, to lead subsequent rounds of financing, a provision that should be approached thoughtfully. If an investment-banking house known only to a few loyal adherents on Wall Street is willing to help out in a first-round financing but at a cost of controlling subsequent rounds, the founder may find that price too stiff. On the other hand, it is unrealistic to expect an investment banker to work enthusiastically on the most difficult financing—that is, the earliest—and then simply take his chances at being remembered with gratitude when subsequent, more lucrative rounds are being discussed.

One value of a placement agent at an early stage is that it will, in all likelihood, impose some important imperatives upon the founder, in some cases to his consternation. For example, experienced corporate financiers save time by introducing founders to the real world of early-stage finance and some of the "rules," such as that all moneys raised go into the company (and none of it leaks out to the founder). Often the founder has built up a debt from the company to himself for accrued and unpaid salary, money loaned, and so forth. With his own creditors knocking at his door, the founder may approach a financing with an eye to intercepting some of the money for himself, to pay his urgent bills. A placement agent will rapidly disabuse a founder of that notion.

VENTURE-CAPITAL CLUBS

One often-tried gambit for raising cash is to make a presentation at a forum organized by a "venture-capital club," referring to an idea first popularized by Thomas Murphy. Venture-capital clubs consist of an organizer and a mailing list of individuals and entities in a given region that have demonstrated some interest in venture capital. There are about seven dozen such groups in the United States; they meet monthly over breakfast or lunch. They usually rely on word of mouth for attendance, as they don't ordinarily advertise. The most important part of a typical meeting is the "Five-Minute Forum," in which anyone can speak about his venture for a limit of one to five minutes. The purported purpose of attending these meetings is for people to make "contacts," not offers.

As the number of venture-capital clubs has increased, so too have the number of schools and associations aimed at helping entrepreneurs in all aspects of starting and running a business. Moreover, some of the venture-capital conferences, such as those sponsored by the American Electronics Association and the celebrated trade shows, provide promising venues for entrepreneurs to meet investors.

CONCEPT IPOS

In some market cycles, including today's savage hunger for internet-related stocks, the interest in high-tech issues is so robust that so-called concept or resumé public offerings are feasible. Feeding frenzies in the public market spotlight certain underwriters who are prepared, on a best-efforts basis, to agree to promote a public offering of securities in a company that has no sales and earnings—only a concept and/or the impressive resumés of its officers and directors. Those underwriters come and go. The names change as some go out of business when the music stops, but a new wave seems ever ready when market conditions warrant. The prospectus of a concept offering will, to be sure, contain Draconian warnings that the offering is "speculative" and involves a "high degree of risk." In the appropriate market environment, however, those warnings often attract rather than repel investors. There are international variations on the theme. Some auction markets—the British Unlisted and the Vancouver Stock Exchange, for example—will admit to trading shares of development-stage companies. Despite the occasional success stories, few if any experienced professionals recommend the premature public offering as a desired strategy, since the burdens of public registration are so significant and the risks of failure are magnified in the public arena; there are fewer excuses and little forgiveness for red ink.

THE SHELL GAME

As the search for equity capital for development-stage entities intensifies, so the collective imagination of managers and financial intermediaries swells to meet the challenge. One of the newer and occasionally popular techniques for raising money is the shell game. The trick is to organize a shell corporation—no assets, no business—and take it public. Because of the unfortunate connotations of the term "shell" in the financial arena, sponsors have developed a more glamorous and respectable label—Specified Purpose Acquisition Companies, or SPACs. The sole purpose of a Shell/SPAC offering is to raise a relatively modest amount of money, and more importantly, to get a number of shares outstanding in the hands of the public. Usually the shares are sold in units; for example, one share of common plus warrants at the current offering price. The sponsors of the shell corporation then find an operating company with which to merge. The merged companies then start reporting the results of operations; if and when those results are promising, the existing stockholders exercise their warrants and pump needed capital into the enterprise. The object of this exercise is, to paraphrase the Red Queen, "public offering first, business operations afterwards"; in that sense it is like a concept offering. But the concept is pure, unsullied by even a business description except to find companies after the IPO with which to merge; warrants (purportedly, at least) supply an evergreen source of financing at attractive prices for the original investors.

Another method, a variation on the shell game, involves the identification of an existing shell or inactive public company (IPC or Newco) as a candidate for a reverse acquisition. A typical example is a company recently emerging from bankruptcy, stripped of its assets other than a modest amount of cash, the assets having been disposed of and the creditors paid in a reorganization proceeding usually labeled a "liquidating Chapter 11." The principal asset of the IPC (other than the cash, if any) is its public registration (although the shares are not then trading on a national market system) and a roster of shareholders.

Transaction expenses are reportedly lower in a reverse acquisition, even after adding in significant post-closing expenses necessary to acquaint the financial community with the business of the newly public firm. Indeed, in the end, the ownership remaining with the shareholders of the target is not supposed to be dramatically different than if an IPO were successful. The latter, however, is supposed to offer speed, greater certainty of completion, less burdensome filing requirements, and independence from general market conditions. Newco's fund-raising effort starts, in fact, after the acquisition closes and Newco's shares are listed. Thus, the acquisition is often accompanied by a bridge loan, a private placement, and/or an offshore offering under Regulation S.

In the case of both SPACs and IPCs, a certain amount of heightened SEC scrutiny can be expected.

MULTIPLE-ROUND STRATEGY

Few, if any, start-ups survive to maturity on the basis of a single round of financing. It is in the nature of the venture-capital beast that companies consume cash in their early stages at unforeseen, sometimes alarming rates. Not only must products be developed, but, in the classic venture-capital scenario, a new market must be penetrated and, indeed, sometimes created. Digital computers, xerography, express mail, the internet—these were not products developed to satisfy the public perception of existing demand. Rather, the existence of the product created—uncovered, if one prefers—the demand; necessity was not the mother of invention. Today it is difficult to see how humanity could get along without these staples. Nonetheless, no customers' queue awaited computers until the computer was introduced and created the queue in the first instance.

Accordingly, the need of a start-up for frequent and regular infusions of cash is an imperative of the business, part of the culture of venture-backed start-ups. A sensible financing strategy focuses not only on the round on the table, but on the impact of subsequent rounds as well. Ultimate dilution of the founder will depend on the success or failure of the company in raising subsequent rounds at higher prices. In considering a given investor's offer, the founder must make a judgment whether the investor has the staying power to support the investment in subsequent periods and will do so at a fair price. Leasing money, in other words, is a longitudinal process; it extends at least until the exit strategy is implemented.

If there is one single enemy encountered by a founder in a venture financing, it is investor indecision and delay. Founders contribute to the problem because they listen selectively, interpreting a politely worded "no" as an invitation to continue with the presentation. To induce investors to declare themselves, one strategy is to line up a lead or "bell cow" investor and hold a first closing, escrowing the proceeds of the offering until enough subscriptions are collected to round out a viable financing. The hope is to create some form of stampede among investors on the fence. At the least, an early closing will serve to freeze the terms and diminish niggling over minor points.

The first round is usually the most dilutive financing, because, obviously, it occurs at the moment of highest risk. Therefore, an intelligent founder will attempt to strike a balance in his first round between obtaining as much money as he thinks he'll need to get to the next stage of development, but not so much that his equity is reduced to the borderline of triviality.

If it is assumed that later rounds will be less dilutive, then it is obvious that the first round should raise the smallest amount of money necessary to take the enterprise to the next round. On the other hand, if money is available, it could be a gross error of judgment not to take it, since the second round may (as it often is) be a good deal more difficult than anticipated, perhaps only because fashions change.

One old saw has it that a start-up firm *never* has enough money, and there are anecdotes in sufficient number to illustrate that proposition. There is, however, contrary evidence, not only to the effect that the first round can be unnecessarily dilutive but that some companies are cursed in their early stages with too much money. For example, a dynamic manager may break away from a company he's helped found and start the process all over again. Since venture investors are no less sheeplike than the rest of us, they extrapolate the past and assume that Mr. Genius can do it again. The founder takes a pregnant idea and money falls in his lap. He's not worried about dilution in the first round because of the valuation he has been able to sell to the investment community. Forgetting the parsimonious habits of his youth, the founder then attempts to shorten the development process by doubling the number of sales and marketing people, putting on more technicians and so forth. He creates a monthly expense outlay, a "burn rate," which is out of proportion to realistic expectations of the company's development. When it comes time for a second round, the existence of a massive burn rate has inexorably postponed the date on when cash break-even will occur by a period which intimidates old and new investors. Only those who have gone through the process know how difficult it is, both logistically and in human terms, to make dramatic slashes in a burn rate. Unsympathetic landlords may refuse to take back the necessary space; firing people imposes separation costs as well as personal trauma.

In short, a higher-than-necessary burn rate is a bad sign, a red flag to the venture-capital community. Founders consistently complain they are being starved by the investors. Fed hand to mouth, they bemoan the opportunities missed for lack of capital; they cite the fact that venture capital is an early-entry strategy. As General Nathan Bedford Forest said, "Get there fustest with the mostest." True in some instances, but the converse is equally likely, based on evidence of the past: Too much money equals potential trouble.

CASE STUDY IN FINDING MONEY: A REALITY CHECK

Mary Jones, a biochemist, has stumbled across an interesting piece of science and has been given the opportunity to license the same by the university for which she works, for a nominal up-front fee, an ongoing royalty, plus a gratis equity position in the company. The principal condition of the license is that the science be exploited commercially. The science, if proven to perform as early indications suggest, will greatly reduce the need for insulin injections by patients suffering from juvenile and adult-onset diabetes. Since diabetes is growing at an alarming rate, particularly among adults, Jones is excited and prepared to quit her job. She is intimidated, however, by the fact the development of the drug through FDA animal and clinical trials may, she understands from individuals who have "been there," cost upwards of $30 to $40 million. Indeed, simply to fund testing to get a new drug ready for the FDA will require several hundred thousands of dollars of additional work in the lab.

Jones goes to the Internet and downloads some of the existing literature on early-stage finance; she puts together a business plan seeking to raise the entire amount necessary to get her product on the market. At this point, the case study is interrupted by a supervening fact: Jones is almost certain to fail. With exceptions with which I am not personally familiar (other than a few extraordinary internet-related examples), it is impossible to raise a multimillion dollar amount of capital for a start-up in one lump sum. If one sets out to do so, time and money are wasted. The successful examples, accordingly, divide the fund-raising process into small bites. The first amount of capital raised (called a "tranche" in VC jargon) is $500,000. There is no magic in that number but it has repeated itself often enough that it has become part of the canon. Five hundred thousand dollars takes the start-up to the point where indications of success have become strong. There is, perhaps, even a so-called beta test, meaning a working prototype of the product or technology and, in the biotech arena, successful phase-one trials. The next tranche is, therefore, $3 million. Again, there is no magic to the number, but it repeats itself so often it has become part of the culture. The $3 million also may come from high net worth individuals, often those acquainted with the founder (and here the jargon is that the founder is going through his or her "Rolodex offering"), but also may include a venture fund, turning the financing into the "first venture round." Getting ahead of the story, the $3 million does not arrive in one lump sum, ordinarily, but in increments. Recognizing that $3 million is only a fraction of the $30 to $40 million needed, the founder and her advisers, perhaps including a boutique placement agent at this stage, are coincidentally searching for strategic investment, for example, a minority tranche from an ethical drug company in exchange for stock, marketing, and distribution rights to the technology if it clicks. Again, the case study indicates the rules of thumb in the trade. The strategic investor invests at a 25 percent more favorable valuation than the financial partners, a number validated by reliable survey materials. But the bad news is that it takes about twice as long for a strategic investor to make up its mind as a financial partner.

The company is then up and operating, slogging its way through the FDA gauntlet of phase-one, phase-two, and phase-three trials, and burning money at a rate of several hundred thousand dollars a month. As the science arrives at the early stages of FDA scrutiny and trials, the VCs and the founder start talking about a megafinancing by tapping the public equity markets—an initial public offering (IPO).

Again, referencing current fashion, serious investment bankers (and not those firms of questionable pedigrees sometimes known as the "Boca Raton" bankers) express an interest conditional on the company having at least one, and preferably more, applications of its science in phase-three trials. The minimum size of the offering is $30 million for somewhere around one-third of the company, meaning a total post-IPO company valuation of $100 million. A financing takes about six months from start to finish and is fraught with risk, including the possibility of a "fail" on the eve of the effective date if the market turns against biotech stocks, as it does episodically for reasons which can be totally unrelated to Jones and her firm. Assuming a successful public offering, $30 million still may not be enough to get to cash-flow break-even, since the company is taking on other scientific projects, which burn money at a rapid rate, in order to justify the expectations of the market that it is a real company and not just a line of one or two products. The IPO is then followed by another primary offering some six months later, assuming the stock holds up well and the market continues to stay in love with the company's prospects. This time the valuation is advanced to, say, $150 million and the company again puts $30 million in its pocket. The period between the first and the second financing is stressful for Jones because she is not only managing her firm but also, once the company has become public, continually spending time cozying up to stockholders, analysts, and other members of the investment community so that the popularity of her company, as measured by the trading price of her stock, remains strong. Jones has been told that the "road show" (that presentation she made to the investment community and investment bankers immediately prior to the IPO) "never ends." The irony is that at a company valuation anywhere under $300 to $500 million, the company risks a visit to the so-called growing orphanage, meaning that cohort comprising 70 percent of the 12,000 companies currently public which are not followed by the investment analysts, and, therefore, are not liquid in any true economic sense, with a stock price reflecting an efficient market. Jones is advised, accordingly, to pursue a so-called rollup or platform strategy, meaning using her public company as the platform to absorb other public and private companies which have not been able to make it on their own but which house interesting science and have brought their intellectual property to the brink of commercial exploitation. By rolling up those companies into her platform, she is able to increase her market capitalization to one-half billion dollars and finally take a one week vacation in the Bahamas.

After all the dilution she still owns about 7 percent of her company personally, which translates, on paper at least, into $35 million. She cannot get out at that price because she is contractually obligated to "lock up" (i.e., not sell) for various periods of time so as not to create undue selling pressure. And, she has been living for four or five years on a salary which is somewhat less than half of what she could have earned had she not entered into this enterprise in the first place. However, she beat the odds. She will ultimately have some liquidity, together with the priceless satisfaction of having grown a major public firm and served mankind in the process. She will no longer, incidentally, be chief executive officer. That post was filled shortly after the first venture round, with Jones continuing as chair and chief scientific officer. The first individual hired having not worked out, there have been two CEOs since: the last one a grizzled veteran of the pharmaceutical industry and a long-time favorite of Wall Street. The office of chief financial officer has also changed hands a couple of times, the law and accounting firms are new, the placement agent was long ago replaced by a major-bracket investment bank. Jones has been sued twice by alleged dissident shareholders—in fact stimulated by underemployed plaintiffs' counsel for allegedly keeping good news (or bad news, depending on how the stock price performed) under wraps for too long. Was it worth it? The answer, of course, depends on the individual. This game is not for everybody.

chapter three

How on Earth Do I Put a Value on My Company?

When a founder determines it is worth his while to attempt to raise money for his concept, the basic issue becomes one of price. If, for example, the business needs $500,000 to get started, how much of the equity in that company should $500,000 in fresh cash command? A brief summary of common terminology will help illuminate the subsequent discussion.

The word "capitalization," or its abbreviation, "cap," is often used in pricing start-ups, with, on occasion, differing meanings. The "market capitalization" or cap of a company refers to the result obtained by multiplying the number of equity shares outstanding by some assigned per-share value. If it has been determined that a share of stock in the company is "worth" $10 and the company has 100,000 shares outstanding, then its market cap is $1 million. The second use of the term has to do with the rate at which future flows are to be valued, a rate sometimes called the "discount" or "cap rate," meaning that that flow of income is to be assigned a one-time value by being "capitalized." Thus, elementary valuation theory teaches that one of the most reliable indicia of value to be assigned to a fledgling (or, indeed, any) enterprise is a number which capitalizes projected income streams. In its simplest form, the question is what an informed investor would pay (i.e., what sum of capital would be put up) in exchange for a promise to pay him annually a certain sum of money. In working out the numbers, it is assumed that the investor wants his capital returned to him, plus a competitive rate of interest. The higher the assumed interest rate (deemed competitive with other investment opportunities), the higher the annual payments must be, given a fixed amount of capital invested on day one. Alternatively, a fixed amount and number of annual payments can be a given element in the formula; the assumed amount of capital to be invested (i.e., the discounted value of the future payments) is then derived, again as a function of the cap rate selected. As the assumed interest or cap rate goes up, the discounted value of the payment stream goes down; fewer dollars are required on day one to earn the investor, at the higher rate, the forecasted income flows.

Another common expression is "before the money" and "after the money." This denotes an ostensibly simple concept, which occasionally trips up even the most sophisticated analysts. If a founder values his company at $1 million on Day 1, then 25 percent of the company is "worth" $250,000—Q.E.D. However, there may be an ambiguity. Suppose the founder and the investors agree on two terms: (1) a $1 million valuation, and (2) a $250,000 equity investment. The founder organizes the corporation, pays a nominal consideration for 1,000 shares, and shortly thereafter offers the investor 250 shares for $250,000. Immediately there can be a disagreement. The investor may have thought that equity in the company was worth $1,000 per percentage point; $250,000 gets 250 out of 1,000—not 1,250—shares. The founder believed that he was contributing to the enterprise property *already* worth $1 million. For $250,000, the investor's share of the resultant enterprise should be 20 percent. The uncovered issue was whether the agreed value of $1 million to be assigned to the company by the founder and investor was *prior to* or *after* the investor's contribution of cash.

In whatever language he chooses, each founder takes on the chore of setting a preliminary valuation on the company for purposes of attracting outside capital. The principal point to be kept in mind is obvious but often overlooked. What the *founder* thinks the company is worth is largely irrelevant at this stage. The decision to go forward has been made, and his effort and resources have by now been pledged to the enterprise based on his expectations of risk and reward. When outside financing is being sought, the critical number is what the founder thinks the universe of *investors* will assign as value to the company. The founder's personal valuation comes into play only if the investment community's assigned value is so much lower than his expectation that he is forced to rethink the question whether the game is worth playing at all.

A number of interesting problems arise when the founder attempts to psychoanalyze the investment community to come up with a number that will prove attractive. In first-round financings there is often, and indeed ordinarily, no track record on which to be conclusive as to value. Moreover, existing assets—plant, machinery, equipment, accounts receivable—are seldom, if ever, meaningful in a first round.

There are almost as many methods of calculating value as there are world religions, since the questions are metaphysical in part and depend on the appetites of the observer. In one of the most common scenarios, a five-year forecast is prepared, the thought being that in the fifth year (assuming the projections are accurate) an exit strategy will be implemented; that is, investors will sell their securities for cash or the securities will become publicly traded, the equivalent of cash. It is usually assumed that the investors will realize their entire return upon implementation of the exit strategy; there will be no interim returns since all revenues will be retained in the business. The valuation formula most often used in connection with the forecast is relatively simple.

An investor plans to invest X dollars in the enterprise today for some to-be-determined percentage of the company's equity. The projections predict the company will enjoy Y dollars of net after-tax earnings as of the day the exit strategy is accomplished; that is, the company is sold or goes public. The analyst then picks a multiple of earnings per share in order to hypothesize what the stock might sell for in a merger or an IPO. Since there is no way of forecasting that multiple, the next best strategy is to use existing multiples in the given industry. What is the PE (ratio of share price to earnings per share) of companies in comparable fields today? Let's assume that multiple to be ten, meaning that the total market capitalization of the company immediately prior to the IPO will be ten times the net earnings for such year. The investor then picks that return on his investment which corresponds to the risk he deems himself encountering, taking into account the return on competing investments, again a subjective judgment. He may believe that he is entitled to a 38-percent compounded rate of return, which means, by rule of thumb in the venture community, that the company forecasts a "five-times" return; that is, the investor will get back, before tax, five dollars for every one dollar invested. If the investment called for is $250,000, then five times $250,000 is $1.25 million. If the company is forecast to be worth $10 million in Year 5, then the investor's $250,000 should command 12.5 percent of the company in Year 1.

Of course, many of the elements of the formula are highly speculative, particularly the reliability of the company's forecast. The method of taking that subjectivity (risk of error) into account is to adjust the rate-of-return target, or "bogey" or "hurdle rate" as it is sometimes called. If the investor thinks the forecast is suspect, one way of sensitizing the equation to his suspicion is to increase the rate of return target from, say, 38 percent to as much as, perhaps, a 50-percent compounded rate of return. If an adjustment has to be made to conjugate a rate of return much higher than 50 percent, then it's arguable the investor should not make the investment in the first place. Because compounded rates of return in excess of 50 percent are so unusual, many investors feel it is unrealistic to predicate an investment on that kind of expectation. The power of compounding is enormous. Many neophytes are inhabiting fantasy worlds when they dream of investments continuing to compound at double-digit rates over an extended period.

PORTFOLIO MANAGEMENT

In considering the issue of valuation generally, one should understand the environment in which a manager of a venture pool operates; he is investing not in one but in a number of opportunities. One of the foundations of modern portfolio theory is the concept that the return on an asset cannot be viewed by itself; rather it must be judged by its contribution to the portfolio as a whole. Thus, when deciding to invest in a company, the venture capitalist must consider how the expected return on the new investment is correlated with the others he holds, ranking opportunities on both an ordinal and cardinal scale. In a significant sense, a cardinal ranking of sorts is always involved because the portfolio manager does not enjoy an infinite array of opportunities. If he is a venture manager, it is incumbent on him to put his money to work in venture investments, meaning that he has to compare each opportunity with what he has and what he is likely to be offered. If a given deal looks like it is better than anything else in sight, he is likely to take it on the founder's terms, even though his own number (based on his idea of valuation in a perfect universe) would be lower were his alternatives wider.

Again in keeping with the idea that it is the portfolio, not the individual investments, being managed, venture capitalists usually diversify their holdings by categories of risk, investing across varying risk levels: a cohort of start-ups carrying, say, an average (forecast) 40-percent compounded rate of return coupled with later-round financings which promise lower returns as a trade-off for better downside protection and the ability to cash out in the near term. Parenthetically, one must recognize that modern portfolio theory cannot be applied uncritically to a venture portfolio because, as one analyst has put it, venture investments "are not available in continuously desirable funding instruments." The new venture manager cannot decide to put 1 percent of the capital pool in a venture that actually needs 6 percent of the pool in order to reach the next development milestone, not unless someone else can be counted on to put up the next installment.

NONNUMERICAL FACTORS

Despite the seeming exactitude of a discounted earnings formula, professional venture managers understand that, because of the enormous uncertainties involved, elaborate valuation techniques are not ends in themselves in venture investing; rather, these techniques are tools, inputs which contribute to (but do not determine) a composite judgment that is based, in the final analysis, on judgment and experience. One can construct elegant models, but if, *au fond*, the result depends ultimately on an informed guess as to future earnings which can be shifted from one end of the plausible range to the other by a factor of 100 percent, mathematical exactitude is trivial, violating the law of significant numbers (multiplying two numbers, one carried out to a single decimal and the other to 10 places). Accordingly, a number of judgmental factors are routinely taken into account in arriving at estimated values.

As an obvious example, the investor must consider the outlook for the industry as a whole, the likely competitive position of the issuer, trends in customer tastes, dependence of the business on a few major customers or suppliers, possible product obsolescence, likely capital needs, the ability to leverage, potential impact of changes in the regulatory climate and so forth. Much attention will focus on likely market share, in part due to the popularity of the Boston Consulting Group's foursquare matrix, which emphasizes market share's influence on a company's ability to become a "cash cow." Valuation based on the discounted value of projected earnings is then adjusted up, down, or sideways depending on the analyst's judgment as to the effect of the nonquantified factors. The outcome is a product only partly of mathematics and principally of judgment and experience.

chapter four

What Legal Form Works Best for You?

W hen a business plan is developed, consideration must be given to the form in which the business is to be conducted. The several possibilities start with a general business corporation, sometimes referred to as a "C Corporation" for that subchapter of the Internal Revenue Code (Subchapter C) which governs the tax attributes of corporations generally. The C Corporation is the residual norm, elected after the other alternatives have been eliminated, the old reliable to which planners turn after exotic formats have been considered and rejected. Before focusing on the corporate form in detail, a discussion of the alternatives is in order.

S CORPORATIONS

A special subtype of the incorporated entity is termed the "S Corporation" (formerly "Subchapter S" Corporation), again the name taken from the location of the governing provisions in the Code. For most purposes, S Corporations are garden-variety corporations under state law, the distinguishing factor being that if they configure themselves to meet special rules of the Internal Revenue Code, no corporate tax is assessed, thereby passing through corporate income and losses directly to the shareholders. Under the Tax Reform Act of 1986, S Corporations became increasingly popular because, for the first time since 1916, personal tax rates were lower than the corporate tax rates, thereby putting a premium on the ability of a business entity to pass through its income to its shareholders without the imposition of tax. Moreover, while losses from passive activities may not be offset against income other than from passive activity under the Tax Reform Act of 1986, losses garnered by an S Corporation and allocable to a shareholder who materially participates—as an officer, for example—in the S Corporation's business may elude the "passive activity" trap and thus be more widely useful. Such losses are, however, limited generally to the shareholder's tax basis in his stock and any loans he has made to the corporation.

The constraints on the structure of S Corporations are relatively rigid and may lead to the ultimate replacement of the vehicle by limited liability companies. The root problem is that Congress contemplated a limited exemption to the obligation to pay corporate tax, benefiting uncomplicated, modestly capitalized businesses.

For present purposes, it is sufficient to note that consideration of the question whether to elect S Corporation status should not stop at the federal tax level. The treatment of S Corporations for local tax purposes can complicate the issue substantially, since some states (and New York City) refuse to recognize S Corporations as "flow-through" entities. Moreover, a large element of any individual or corporate tax strategy has to do with the treatment of fringe benefits. A person owning 2 percent or more of the voting stock of an S Corporation is a "partner" for certain fringe-benefit purposes—for example, group term life insurance and medical insurance—and a partner still fares less well in the fringe-benefit area than does a stockholder/employee of a C Corporation.

The good news is that S Corporation status is relatively easy to achieve and, when the circumstances warrant, to surrender; a timely election approved by the shareholders and filed with the IRS is all that is required. There are constraints, as one would expect, in attempting to manipulate S Corporation status—that is, if a C Corporation builds up unrealized appreciation in its assets and then switches to S status prior to a sale of those assets in order to avoid double tax, the IRS has statutory weapons. However, it appears that the S Corporation device can be a useful technique to escape an "excess of accumulated earnings" problem.

A final word: many small, closely held corporations need not (and should not) bother with filing for S Corporation status; to avoid double tax, the management may simply pay out all the profits each year in year-end bonuses. If the company needs to retain earnings, the key managers can make loans back to the company, the company paying (and deducting) interest at the "federal rate" (the rate a loan must carry to avoid taxes on assumed interest). In fact, a company owned solely by shareholder/employees can wind up paying more tax if it elects S over C status. However, there are problems in pursuing the task of distributing all earnings in a venture context. If the founder is trying to bail out some day at a multiple of historical earnings, the clean-out-the-store approach leaves a slim trail of earnings to which a high multiple can attach. When such businesses are bought and sold, the income statement can be recreated pro forma, but the very fact an explanation is required may put the founder at a disadvantage in negotiating price.

LIMITED LIABILITY COMPANIES

The limited liability company, in effect an incorporated partnership, has gained considerable momentum since 1988, when the Internal Revenue Service ruled that a corporation organized under a special Wyoming statute qualified for pass-through tax treatment as a partnership even though the entity possessed the corporate characteristic of limited liability. The following discussion of the anatomy of a limited liability company is oriented toward the Delaware statute (the Act). In the following discussion, it should be assumed that unless otherwise indicated or unless the context suggests otherwise (i.e., fundamental rules on how the entity is to be organized), any provision of the Act can be modified by agreement of the parties.

Under the law in some states, a limited liability company must have at least two "members" (i.e., owners), an inheritance from the underlying concept of liability company which implies two or more participants. As a structuring issue, query whether, if only two partners are involved, the agreement between them should not name a mutually acceptable third party to become a member if one member dies or withdraws, if only for purposes of liquidating the entity.

The members may directly manage the company or they may delegate all or a portion of that task to "managers" (the limited liability company equivalent of directors or general partners). Limited liability companies can be organized in Delaware for any purpose other than banking or insurance.

A limited liability company is formed by filing a certificate of formation with the secretary of state. The certificate must set forth the name of the company (which shall contain the words "Limited Liability Company" or "LLC"), the address of its registered office, and the name and address of its registered agent for service of process. As opposed to statutes in other states, the certificate need not identify the names and business addresses of the initial members or managers, nor the purposes for which the LLC was organized. The omission of members' and/or managers' names is clearly the better practice. The list of limited partners required in the certificate by outdated versions of the Uniform Limited Partnership Act only served to identify prospects for salesmen pushing securities; if identification is required, publicity-shy members will employ dummies.

The Act contemplates that the affairs and conduct of the business of a limited liability company will be governed by a written operating agreement (the Agreement). There is no requirement that the Agreement be made public; some practitioners may, however, wish to publicize portions of the Agreement, by incorporating the same in the Certificate of Formation, in hopes that constructive notice to, say, creditors and vendors, will prove helpful at some point down the road. If an LLC is to be used as a special-purpose, bankruptcy-remote vehicle, for example, the sponsors might want a purpose clause on the public record indicating to all the world that the company is *not* authorized to borrow money or run up bills except in certain specified ways.

The Agreement may contain any provisions for the regulation and management of the company which are not inconsistent with the Act. The entity may be governed democratically like a general partnership, all members voting on all matters in proportion to their profits' interests, with no delegation to managers. However, the norm is expected to be delegation of management functions to managers (a.k.a. directors). The Act does not, parenthetically, mention officers specifically; but there is no reason not to appoint the same if deemed useful, much as partnerships appoint officers from time to time.

The Agreement will generally specify how profits and losses will be allocated and distributions made. An important query at this point is whether the Agreement should be like a typical partnership agreement in providing for such items as adjustments to keep the system in sync with the Treasury Regulations under I.R.C. §704 (e.g., minimum-gain charge-backs), the appropriate profit allocation upon a distribution in-kind, and the like.

Once a Delaware limited liability company has creditors, no distributions or returns of capital can be made if that action would cause the fair value of its net assets to be less than zero. Indeed, under applicable fraudulent-conveyance statutes, the constraint on distributions extends to those which might make the firm insolvent or leave it unreasonably short of capital. Other than that restriction, however, distributions by a limited liability company can be structured in any way the members or managers choose. If no allocation is specified in the Agreement, the Act specifies that distributions and profits and losses will be allocated by proportionate share of the "agreed value" of membership interests. But discriminatory distributions are allowed if the governing documents so provide. If a member resigns, he is entitled to receive within a reasonable time the fair value of his membership interest based on his right to share in distributions. (A reminder: as indicated above, this and most other rights can be modified or curtailed by the Agreement.)

This Act also clarifies relationships between members and the company. It is, for example, acceptable for a member to transact business with the company. In such a role, the member has the same rights as any nonmember. And, to the extent members have a right to distributions, they enjoy creditor status. Furthermore, it appears managers can be exculpated up to maximum limits one can imagine, absent their actual, knowing, and willful fraud.

The Act specifies that new members may be admitted only with the unanimous consent of the existing members unless the Agreement otherwise provides. And, the Agreement may provide, presumably, just about any admission procedure imaginable; thus, under the Act, one can become a member by orally agreeing to become a member. Stock or other certificates are not specifically mentioned. Moreover, unlike corporations in some states, membership interests can be issued for whatever consideration the members choose, including a promissory note or future services. At this point, of course, careful counsel will consider creating formalities in the Agreement so that, for example, when the time rolls around for an opinion to issue on, say, the status of certain issues, the lawyer concerned will have something to go on.

The Act has established a procedure whereby limited liability companies organized in other jurisdictions can qualify to do business in Delaware. And, the Act is specific on such issues as the LLC's ability to merge with LLCs and C Corporations (foreign and domestic). The Act provides for partnership-type rights of members to look at the books and lists of members, subject only to "reasonable" limitations.

Clearly, limitation of liability for members is a cornerstone of the Act. Members of limited liability companies are not risking their personal assets; they are not liable to creditors "solely by reason of being a member or acting as a manager." Members are, on the other hand, liable for any contributions they agreed in writing to make and the obligation survives death or disability; if required property or services are not contributed, the company may require a cash contribution of equal value. The Act also recognizes that there are contractual elements to the relationship of the members. For example, the Act allows a member or manager to resign unless the Agreement provides he may not, in which case the company may recover damages for breach from the manager (no mention of the member) and offset those damages from other distributions. The Act imposes liability on managers and members to return improper distributions, but, in the case of members, only if the member knew at the time the distribution was improper.

It is likely that, barring unusual circumstances, the interest of a member in an LLC will be deemed to be a "security" under the test laid down in the landmark Supreme Court's *SEC v. Howey* decision and its progeny. In the event of bankruptcy of an LLC, the odds are that the rules pertaining to corporations (versus liability company) will apply. Most states (Florida being a prominent exception) treat LLCs as liability companies for tax purposes.

One major drawback is, of course, the risk that a court outside Delaware considering an action against a Delaware LLC will in effect "pierce the veil" and hold the members and/or managers liable as general partners. The risk is reduced since all states have adopted limited liability company legislation. Moreover, if the sponsors of the LLC observe the customary and usual rules to avoid the corporate veil being pierced, the risk of an LLC being treated as a general partnership should be manageable. We have lived for many years with a similar specter in organizing Massachusetts Business Trusts—to date without significant incident, despite troublesome language in idiosyncratic jurisdictions like Texas.

CORPORATION VERSUS LIMITED LIABILITY COMPANY

There are a number of alternatives not discussed in this text . . . general and limited partnerships, business trusts, sole proprietorships, etc. In the final analysis, the choice of entity usually comes down to an election between a corporation, whether S corporation or C corporation, and a limited liability company. The following is a summary of certain important issues.

Liquidity

Public trading in shares of corporate stock is perceived by most practitioners as easier—that is, more efficiently accomplished —than trading in limited liability company interests. Corporate shares were designed to be liquid; not so limited liability company interests.

Flexibility versus Formality

Except to the extent the general corporation law of a given state provides relief, corporate existence entails a higher degree of formality (and therefore, expense) than life under a limited liability company. Corporations require a formally elected board of directors, statutory officers, stockholders meetings, class votes on certain issues, and records of meetings. These formalities are often neglected, but at some peril; if there is no evidence of formal directors' meetings, plaintiffs can contend the board was ipso facto negligent in carrying out its fiduciary duties to the stockholders because one of the functions of a board is to hold formal meetings.

Familiarity

Corporate law has been more thoroughly developed than limited liability company law in the litigated cases. There is more predictability, accordingly, from a legal standpoint. Counsel can forecast with a higher degree of confidence what the leading oracles on corporate law—the Chancery and Supreme Courts in Delaware—will do on a given state of facts. Indeed, for every case construing a Limited Liability Company Act, there are hundreds construing the general corporation laws. The schizophrenic nature of a liability company—now an entity, now just a see-through label for an aggregate of individual partners—makes for potential confusion.

Tax Issues Influencing the Choice

Organizational tax issues will revolve principally around the fact that earnings by a business operated in corporate form generate federal and state income tax on the corporate level. When those earnings are distributed (if they are) by way of dividends (or in liquidation), they ordinarily generate additional tax again, this time levied upon the shareholders, and such dividends are not deductible corporate expenses. Avoidance of "double taxation" will drive the preference of planners toward the liability company format. There are, to be sure, ways to avoid double taxation, but the gate is substantially narrower than it was pre–January 1, 1987.

The tax issues are extremely complicated, and no attempt will be made to set them out in detail. Much depends on facts and circumstances in a given case interacting with special rules, such as the exclusion from taxable income of a large portion (70 percent, down from 85 percent) of corporate dividends paid to corporate shareholders. This discussion will outline only *general* principles, to be used as guides in analyzing particular cases. To get into the subject in detail a number of code provisions must be analyzed carefully—for example, the new rules restricting the ability of corporations to carry forward net operating losses and the application of alternative minimum tax to corporations.

Starting one's business in noncorporate form will prove to be popular for yet another reason. Upward pressure on corporate rates, plus the post-1986 difficulty in extracting profits from corporate solution without paying double tax, puts a premium on avoiding corporate tax altogether. It is true that partners pay tax on revenue whether it is distributed or not and it may be necessary to retain earnings in the entity to expand the business. That is not, however, a major problem in most instances. The limited liability company simply distributes enough cash to the partners to pay tax at an assumed rate (28 to 34 percent, plus something for state taxes) and retains the rest, the danger being that the limited liability company will have taxable income but no cash, in a year of large principal payments on debt, for example.

Migration from one form of organization to another is a one-way street. A limited liability company can organize a corporation and transfer its assets thereto without tax, assuming that the partners contributing cash and/or the property hold 80 percent or more of the resultant voting stock and the liabilities of the limited liability company do not exceed the fair value of its assets; if a corporation wants to organize itself as a limited liability company, however, there is a double tax under the new tax law. Appreciated assets are taxed at the corporate level and the shareholders taxed on the liquidation distributions.

Further, election of the limited liability company structure allows somewhat greater flexibility in allocating items of income and loss among the partners. The dream of the organizers of a business is to be able to strike a deal between the suppliers of capital and the managers in a tax-neutral setting. The founder and the investors want to be able to arrange the split between them of calls on the company's future income (in the person of shares of capital stock or interests in limited liability company profits) without worrying about the consequences of that allocation as a taxable event to either party. In a limited liability company, interests in profits can be allocated and reallocated more or less as the parties agree, without regard to the respective contributions of capital. The allocation must have "substantial economic effect," which means not much more than that a scheme directly keyed to the tax status of the partners is questionable. A corporation can distribute stock disproportionate to paid-in capital but only within certain limits.

On the other hand, limited liability companies are not eligible to participate in tax-postponed reorganizations under I.R.C. §368. Because a limited liability company can be incorporated without tax, that problem may not be insuperable, but attempts to incorporate a limited liability company on the eve of a statutory merger could run afoul of the "step transaction" test. Moreover, venture funds usually will not invest in LLCs because such investments create intractable tax problems for certain of their own investors . . . tax-exempt pension and endowment funds and offshore investors.

Finally, one of the most significant disadvantages of a LLC is associated with the issuance of membership interests to employees of a LLC upon exercise of employee options. Generally, the grant of an option to purchase LLC equity to an employee does not have an immediate taxable consequence for the LLC or the employee. However, upon the exercise of such an option by an employee, who then becomes a holder of LLC equity, several significant tax consequences appear likely. Although the issue is not free from doubt, once an employee acquires LLC equity, he or she is likely to be treated as a partner for tax purposes.

One fairly straightforward solution is to forestall option exercises until after the date the LLC converts to a C corporation in anticipation of an IPO or acquisition or merger. Options would "vest" under a schedule to be determined, but would not be exercisable until the "first exercise date." For option holders who leave employment prior to this first exercise date, the post-termination exercise period would continue until the conversion of the LLC. By extending the post-termination exercise period, no departing employee will feel compelled to exercise the option that would otherwise expire due to termination of employment. Preventing option exercises also will save the LLC the costs associated with accounting and reporting obligations to a holder of a relatively small interest in the LLC. It also simplifies the management of the LLC when membership votes are required.

The complexity of the analysis—corporation versus limited liability company—is multiplied by the fact that there are issues other than federal income tax to take into account, including the impact of state taxes, medical insurance, and other nontrivial expenses. There is, in the final analysis, only one way in which to illuminate and decide the most intelligent election between the corporate and the limited liability company form. Take the business forecast and run two scenarios: limited liability company versus corporation. Compare the after-tax wealth of the shareholders assuming, say, a sale of their shares in Year 5 at a multiple of ten times earnings. Look at the difference and decide.

chapter five

What Will My Corporation Look Like?

A ssuming corporate status is elected, what will the animal look like? This chapter outlines some of the principal attributes.

A corporation is an artificial legal entity chartered by one of the fifty states and endowed by the legislature with certain valuable privileges; it follows that its powers are limited to those expressly or impliedly set out by statute. With exceptions not generally significant, a corporation is managed by its directors.

The general corporation laws in each state vary in detail, but they follow a generally similar pattern. The Model Revised Business Corporation Act, drafted by a select committee of the American Bar Association, is a composite of the most advanced thinking.

CORPORATE CHARTER

A corporation is created by the preparation and filing of a document entitled the "certificate of incorporation" or "charter." This is the fundamental, organic document governing the relationships among the various interests of the officers, directors, shareholders, and creditors. Since the charter predates the existence of directors or stockholders, it is signed by individuals known as incorporators, often personnel in the incorporating lawyer's office. A number of significant issues, detailed in the following sections, are encountered at an early stage—that is, when the charter is drafted.

Name

By statute and under the common-law principles of unfair competition, the corporation may not adopt a name which is deceptively similar to the name of an existing corporation either incorporated under the laws of, or duly qualified to do business in, a given state. Further, most statutes require that the corporation signify its incorporated status by including in its name words such as "Corporation," "Corp.," "Ltd.," or "Inc." The state secretary's office maintains a list of all domestic corporations and all foreign corporations registered to do business in the state. By perusing the list, a founder or his counsel can see whether a given name has already been taken. If a multistate operation is contemplated, certain agents—for example, the CT Corporation System—will search the rosters of the important commercial states to see if a given name is available. It is usually possible to reserve a name in most states for up to ninety days. The exclusive use of the name is then nailed down by formally going through the process of qualifying to do business as a foreign corporation in that state. The name of the corporation (versus the trade name) is not always critical; if the name Biodynamics has already been taken, for example, the state secretary will usually accept the name of, say, "Bio-dynamics Informatics." Hence, a right to reserve a corporate name by qualifying to do business in a number of states is not usually a justified (in view of the expense) strategy for a start-up. If, however, the corporate name is to be used as the distinctive name under which goods are to be sold to consumers, a search and registration procedure qualifying the name as part of a distinctive trademark or trade name should be conducted under the federal trademark law, known as the Lanham Act.

Par Value of Stock

The charter denominates the par value of each share of common and preferred stock, the number of shares of each class of stock authorized, and the various rights and privileges of each class of stock. The original purpose of a stated par value was to protect the creditors of the corporation by requiring that the consideration for the shares issued equal at least their aggregate par value and that the capital equivalent of the number of shares issued times the par value of each share be permanent capital of the corporation, not subject to decrease by voluntary acts of the directors in favor of the stockholders, such as dividends or repurchases of shares. While creditors no longer rely, if they ever did, on the stated capital of a corporation, it remains customary to assign each share a nominal par value (versus no-par stock) and allocate the remaining consideration paid for the issuance of shares to a "paid-in" surplus account generally available for dividends and redemptions. Although no-par value shares are legally possible, it is often advisable to issue shares at some par value—say one cent versus no-par value—because the franchise tax and annual license fees in many states are tied to the number of outstanding shares valued at their par value and no-par shares may be assigned a par value of as much as one dollar.

PAYMENT FOR STOCK

An atavistic desire to protect creditors explains why state statutes continue to regulate the types of consideration for which corporate stock can be issued. Cash and property are eligible, but promissory notes are questionable ("no" in Massachusetts, "yes" in Delaware), and stock rarely may be issued for future services. The trick, of course, is to designate some form of eligible consideration in the minutes— intellectual "property" instead of services, for example. Alternatively, if stock is to be paid in installments and a promissory note is not eligible consideration under state law, it may be possible to work with the concept of assessable stock, stock issued under the provisions of state law which authorize partly paid stock to be issued, subject to calls for further payments.

PURPOSES

The charter requires a statement of the purpose(s) for which the corporation is organized, a section into which the draftsmen were once accustomed to pour a good deal of care. Recent usage, however, supports the practice of making brief mention of the principal purpose of the corporation and then tagging on a line authorizing the corporation to engage in any business in which a corporation organized in the state may lawfully engage. Such "basket" language is now thought adequate to overcome any objection that a particular corporate activity is *ultra vires* (beyond the power of the corporation) because no specific mention thereof has been made in the charter.

When investors or creditors wish to restrain a corporation from roaming far afield, negative covenants in a loan or stock purchase agreement are deemed more flexible than charter provisions.

MISCELLANEOUS CHARTER PROVISIONS

The charter lists the principal place of business and the names and addresses of the initial officers and directors of the corporation. It does not require that the stockholders be identified. If the corporation is organized by a law firm, it is customary to file the papers using "dummy" officers and directors—the "dummies" being employees of the law office involved—and make the necessary changes at the initial shareholders and directors meetings. Some states insist that each corporation have at least three directors and that the charter name at least three officers: for example, president, treasurer, and clerk or secretary. The more modern statutes now allow a corporation to exist with as few as one director (in some states, close corporations may operate with none), and the founder can hold all the offices: the sole director, president, treasurer, clerk or secretary. There are, on occasion, curious local requirements, such as that the clerk be a resident of the state in which the corporation is domiciled; again, modern statutes omit such anachronisms.

The charter is deemed to be a contract between the state and the incorporators, a public document available to inspection by all. Therefore, its provisions can, by virtue of one of the many handy fictions through which the law operates, be deemed binding on all the world, including everybody who takes an interest in the corporation subsequent to the publication of the charter. There is no other instrument with this all-encompassing effect, and, therefore, a careful drafter will load up the charter with those provisions meant to be universally effective. Such provisions are known as "optional" provisions since they are in addition to the material the corporation must provide if the charter documents are to be accepted for filing. They are, however, optional in name only; if no mention is made in the charter, the law may either insert a given provision automatically or deny its right to exist outside the charter. As indicated below, the competent planner makes sure he understands the difference.

RESTRICTIONS ON TRANSFER

In some states, agreements respecting the corporation's power to restrict the transfer of its shares, once issued, are not deemed to be effective unless they are set out in the charter (and, like all restrictions, "legended" upon the face of the share certificates themselves); moreover, any agreement purporting to bind shareholders not signatories to the agreement may only be legally effective if set out in the charter. The typical restriction, in the nature of a first-refusal option, is a significant element of governance in closely held corporations, important to ensure that stock not fall into the hands of strangers without an opportunity in the company (or the remaining shareholders) to buy back some or all of the shares. In small companies, the shareholders feel the need to relate to each other as partners and a maverick shareholder can be disruptive. Moreover, certain valuable privileges, for example S Corporation status, can be forfeited by the wrong transfer.

Well-drafted charter provisions set out a first option on all proposed transfers, whether voluntary or involuntary, and including insolvency, divorce, incompetence, and death. The list should be specific and comprehensive, since courts may construe any restrictions on alienability narrowly. The provisions usually contemplate a repurchase by the company (if the company so elects) at either a price fixed in advance, at a price varying according to a formula (i.e., book value or an earnings multiple), at a price that matches the price offered by a third party, or at "fair value." There are a number of drafting points to keep in mind; for example, whether the first option applies to pledges (when stock is technically transferred, albeit only as collateral); how "fair value" is established in the case of disputes (by arbitrators picked at the time of the disagreement, by named experts such as the company's accountants); whether the party seeking the transfer, if also a director, may vote in favor or against the company's election to exercise its option; and what sanctions (loss of dividends and voting rights) may be imposed and enforced if the shares are transferred against the restriction. Often there are permitted groups—for example, family members and trusts, related corporations—among which shares can be transferred without triggering the option, assuming the transferee independently accepts the restriction.

First-option restrictions should collapse by their own terms upon the pendency of an initial public offering, since the underwriters and the purchasing public will brook no such encumbrance on the liquidity of the public shares. Restrictions of this nature are to be differentiated from so-called investment-letter restrictions, which evidence the illiquidity of unregistered shares and "buy–sell" restrictions designed to recapture stock when an employee terminates. Charter provisions respecting first-refusal restraints should be compared with similar provisions found in the Shareholders Agreement relating to the rights of other shareholders to a preview of any proposed sales. Sometimes first-option restrictions are exercisable by the corporation, and, if it elects to pass, the restrictions segue to the stockholders.

Finally, it should be noted that the discussion of transfer restrictions in the venture-capital context deals with restrictions to which the stockholders have agreed, at least constructively, when they bought stock in corporations with such restrictions in place. An entirely different set of considerations is involved in attempts by management of besieged public companies to impose ex post facto restrictions on publicly held shares so as to disenfranchise intruders.

With the various changes recently enacted into law, it is becoming apparent to the planners of an early-stage enterprise that control of the number and nature of shareholders is a matter of cardinal importance. The issuer actively should manage that list through the imposition of restrictions on transfer, an imperative in light of the various events that could go wrong if control of the list is lost. Thus, uncontrolled transfers may produce the following:

1. A loss of S Corporation status once the S Corporation surpasses the number of shareholders test.

2. Net operating loss carry forwards under §382 of the Code will be reduced if more than 50 percent of the ownership changes hands in a three-year period.

3. Inadvertent status as an investment company might ensue to issuers which have lost the exemption under §3(c)(1) of the Investment Company Act for issuers with fewer than one hundred shareholders.

4. Inadvertent status as a public company under §12(g) of the Securities and Exchange Act of 1934 will eventuate if, in addition to total assets exceeding $1 million, the issuer has outstanding a class of equity security held of record by five hundred or more persons.

5. Avoidance of tax on initial corporate organization through §351 can be lost by reason of ownership shifts immediately after such organization.

The need to patrol transfers can only increase as the lawmakers are increasingly prone to contemplate a corporate world divided into two categories: big and small businesses. Note in this connection that the number of shareholders in an issuer can change by reason of transactions that initially may not have been contemplated as "transfers" when the restrictions were being drafted. For example, if a class of redeemable preferred stock is issued, the redemption of those shares may push an issuer over the 50-percent change in ownership threshold and threaten net-operating-loss carry forwards.

PREFERRED STOCK PROVISIONS

The typical statute requires that the rights and privileges of each class of stock be set out in the charter, meaning and including the preferred stock agreement, unless authority is delegated to the board of directors to fix the terms of the preferred stock on such basis as the board shall deem appropriate at the time of issuance, thereby creating so-called blank-check preferred. Practitioners have generally elected to leave the details of the preferred stock to the directors, the exact drafting to take place when the occasion arises to issue the stock. Blank-check preferred has acquired a pejorative gloss recently since it has become significant in the public corporation arena as an antitakeover (or "shark repellent") provision. Nonetheless, it remains convenient for most start-ups to pursue the less cumbersome course: let the directors fix the terms. If the investors want a say in fixing the terms of the preferred stock to be issued in the future, the thought is that they should so provide by agreement.

PREEMPTIVE RIGHTS

Preemptive rights as such are designated by statute as proper charter provisions since they are part of the "rights and privileges" of a given class of stock. Such rights mean what the name implies: that the existing shareholders of the company have a right to subscribe to any new issuance of shares in such proportions as will maintain their equity position in the company before shares may be offered outside of the existing shareholder group. Again, rights in the nature of preemptive rights are often bargained for by investors but usually not as a charter provision. Once inserted in the charter, they can only be eliminated, as they must when an initial public offering occurs, by a vote of the shareholders, indeed, by a vote of each class of shareholders affected. The investors bargaining for preemptive rights usually want to be able to trigger or waive those rights on their own, so that the Stock Purchase Agreement is the more likely home for provisions of this nature. Planners should be careful to inspect the corporation law of the domicile to ascertain whether the statute is of the "opt in" or "opt out" variety; whether, if the charter is silent (i.e., the organizers do not make a conscious election), cumulative voting or preemptive rights are or are not in effect. Silence is a choice; the trick is to make sure it is a conscious choice.

INDEMNIFICATION

The Revised Model Act provides perhaps the most extensive and best-considered provisions on indemnification by the corporation of directors and officers to be found in any codification. Indemnification provisions may be drafted either in the charter or bylaws, but one school of thought, to which this author subscribes, will place them in the charter so as to provide maximum dignity to often controversial provisions. The ultimate belt-and-suspenders approach includes the practice of executing a contract between the corporation and each director, providing that the director has a specific contractual right to be indemnified.

The issues involved in drafting indemnification provisions are complex and significant, particularly since the ability of start-ups to attract first-class directors is inhibited by the universal unavailability of liability insurance at affordable prices. Indeed, the indemnification provisions in a significant sense set the statutory standard of conduct to which directors are to be held, assuming the corporation is solvent; if a director is to be indemnified in every action he takes or omits unless he is ultimately adjudged "grossly negligent," then the standard has been established for directors: "Do what you want as long as your conduct is not grossly negligent (or worse)."

Few difficulties are presented if a director is sued and ultimately wins, that is, is exonerated. Under any conjugation of the law of indemnification, that director is entitled to be made whole by the corporation for his reasonable expenses. The Revised Model Act and the Delaware statute provide for mandatory indemnification in such cases; unless the charter otherwise provides, the directors must be indemnified. However, most suits, particularly so-called strike suits (actions brought for purposes of badgering the corporation into paying legal fees), are settled prior to judgment; the company pays some modest amount on behalf of its directors but no admission or determination is made—other than the implicit force of a settlement—that anyone has done anything wrong.

A further problem arises when the strike suit is brought in the name of the corporation; that is, a derivative action. The theory of the derivative action is that the directors have violated their duties to the corporation—looted it, in the strongest case—and recovery should go to the corporation. (Strike suit counsel usually bring their complaints as either derivative or class actions, or both, so that the damages claimed—for the benefit of the corporation or all the shareholders as a class—are large enough to get someone's attention. Were counsel limited to claiming damages only on behalf of the shareholders they have recruited as plaintiffs, the damages would be trivial.) If a settlement is reached, the cash paid, over and above attorneys' fees, goes to the corporate treasury; if the corporation pays that money out as indemnification, the process is circular.

Moreover, when a suit is filed and the directors scramble for counsel, fees mount rapidly; arguably, since there is always the possibility the directors will lose in a big way (judged liable for actual fraud, for instance), the company should hold off paying out any money until the outcome is known. On the other hand, good defense lawyers do not work for free; indeed, their fees could impoverish some directors and blackmail them into settling.

The SEC has further confused matters by expressing the view that any indemnification of a director for expenses in settling a claim that the securities laws have been violated (an almost universally encountered claim in the pleadings, if only because it gets counsel into federal court where the activist judges lurk) is against public policy.

Outside the mandatory case—that is, the defendants win—the issues are touchy, particularly since those directors who authorize indemnification payments (usually those not initially sued) are naturally concerned about getting sued themselves by reason of that action. The modern statutes (e.g., the Revised Model Act and Delaware statute) take some of the heat off by dealing expressly with many of the problems. Thus directors can advance to their defendant colleagues or themselves payments of legal fees and expenses against an undertaking to restore the same if found ultimately liable. In a derivative action, directors can be reimbursed for amounts paid as expenses (i.e., plaintiff's counsel fees) but not for any cash paid to the corporation, meaning that derivative actions (unless a policy of insurance is in force) are rarely settled for amounts in excess of counsel fees.

Since a settlement leaves the issue of culpability hanging in the air, the Delaware statute sets out the test to be applied: a director's "good faith" and a "reasonable belief" that his actions were in, or not opposed to, the best interests of the corporation. If the director is deemed to pass this test, then he may be indemnified; indeed, even if he does not settle and a court or jury holds him liable on some sort of negligence theory which does not undercut his good faith or the reasonableness of his belief. If the director is found to have improperly received a personal benefit at the expense of the corporation, good faith is conclusively negated.

The standard of conduct—for that is what it amounts to—has been significantly alleviated in Delaware by the legislature, presumably in an attempt to reverse the quixotic holding in the *Van Gorkom* case, a Delaware Supreme Court opinion so harsh and unreasonable on the directors concerned that it threatened to end Delaware's near-monopoly as the state of preferred incorporation. The basic amendment allows shareholders to limit director exposure by approving a specific clause in the articles of incorporation eliminating liability for breaches of fiduciary duty excepting only:

> [A] breach of the duty of loyalty, for acts or omissions not in good faith or which involve intentional misconduct or a knowing violation of law, for an unlawful payment of dividends or unlawful stock purchases or redemptions, or for any transaction from which the director derived an improper personal benefit.

This is a provision which simply MUST be adopted in the charter; it is not automatic. Failure to accept the legislature's invitation to protect the board is inexcusable.

For the planner charged with drafting the appropriate charter provision, the task is clear: insert into the articles or bylaws either a provision that goes at least as far as the statute, repeating and/or paraphrasing the statutory language, or an authorization of indemnification "to the fullest extent allowable by law." However, since the statute in many states does not by its terms exhaust the comfort which the charter or bylaws can provide, it is advisable to conjure up additional instances where indemnification is authorized—namely, partial indemnification, coverage of former directors, payment of expenses in seeking indemnification, etc.

Finally, indemnification of directors is not an adequate answer to the concerns of directors of early-stage companies; if the company is not solvent, then the indemnification provisions, of course, are nugatory. Consequently, in the appropriate instance, the directors may seek personal indemnification from the founder and/or solvent investors, coupled with specific promises by the founder and other managers of the corporation not to do certain things that might expose the directors to liability. For instance, the directors are liable personally if withheld taxes are not paid to the government; indeed, there can be criminal penalties. Further examples include chapter 151A §71(A) of Massachusetts General Laws, the Plant Closing Law, which requires a notice if any plant located in Massachusetts employing more than forty-nine employees plans to close; liability for failure to notify is imposed on the directors. Various state and environmental statutes, as well as failure to provide health insurance for employees, may impact on the directors personally.

BYLAWS

The typical corporation statute authorizes the directors or the stock-holders (or the incorporators prior to the date stock is issued) to adopt bylaws. These are usually canned documents which rephrase, and fill gaps in, the statutory rules of governance. They are equivalent, in a sense, to *Robert's Rules of Order*: they specify how meetings of directors and stockholders are called, what constitutes a quorum, and what votes are necessary to adopt a motion. They set out such matters as the corporation's fiscal year, the time and place of the annual meeting, standing committees of the board and their powers, the duties of principal executive officers, and, of course, how the bylaws are to be amended. In some closely held companies, the scope of each executive's duties and powers may be the subject of intense negotiations; the bylaw provisions should be drafted to reflect the organizers' intent, consistent with the substantive provisions on this point in the Stockholders Agreement and/or each officer's employment contract. It is embarrassing to find one description of the president's duties in that agreement, drafted after elaborate negotiations, and another in a boilerplate paragraph in the bylaws.

In the author's view—with which some practitioners differ—the bylaws are not, as a matter of good practice, the place in which important substantive matters are to be placed; that privilege belongs to the charter or to agreements among the company and specific shareholders. The bylaws contain the nuts and bolts, procedural regulations which smooth the way for the company to operate. They are largely repetitive of the statute and can be amended by the directors without shareholder consent. The bylaws are not on the public record.

OTHER ORGANIZATIONAL DOCUMENTS

Minutes of First Meeting

The minutes of the first meeting of directors are a significant organizational document. At that meeting a number of administrative details are taken care of: the forms of stock certificate and corporate seal are adopted; the initial stock issuances are authorized; bank resolutions are passed; special committees of the board, if any, are constituted and directors appointed to the same; and additional officers—that is, vice presidents, assistant treasurers—are appointed.

Stock Book

Of cardinal importance is the stock record book, since it tracks critical information: who owns what number of shares. Under Article 8 of the Uniform Commercial Code (UCC), in effect in all important commercial states, the issuance and transfer of shares are monitored by an institution known as a transfer agent. For large, publicly held companies, the transfer agent is usually a bank or trust company, computerized and staffed to record millions of transactions a day. Start-up companies, dealing with a limited number of stockholders, act as their own transfer agents; they (or their counsel) maintain the stock record book themselves.

For some reason, the stock book is often the least carefully maintained of the important legal records, a troublesome slip since stock certificates, the counterpart record of outstanding shares, are often misplaced by the recipients, and despite the fact that the Code requires a bond (usually in an amount equal to twice market value) to indemnify the company against damage in the event a stock certificate is lost. (In its discretion, the issuer may waive a corporate surety and accept the shareholder's individual indemnity, the usual practice in closely held companies.) More importantly, when the need comes for counsel's opinion concerning the number of shares outstanding—as in connection with the sale of the company, a merger, or an initial public offering—an enormous amount of reconstructive attention often has to be paid to the stock record book.

STATE OF CORPORATE DOMICILE: DELAWARE OR SOMEWHERE ELSE?

If the corporate form is selected, the next issue is where best to be domiciled. Ordinarily one would minimize expense by incorporating the business in the state in which the business is to be conducted, thereby saving the cost of appointing an agent in, say, Delaware, the most popular state for those seeking a flag of convenience. (There is rarely an income-tax advantage to domiciling a business outside of its principal place of operations; the income of a business operated in Massachusetts will generally be subjected to the same Massachusetts income tax whether it is technically a Massachusetts or a Delaware corporation.) Engaging a firm of professional representatives such as the Corporation Trust Company to act as resident agent in Delaware entails a modest, but not so trivial, fee each year. On the other hand, the Delaware corporate statute is well drafted and contains few of the anomalies one finds, on occasion, in the general corporation laws of certain other states. Moreover, the Delaware state secretary's office is well staffed and Delaware bureaucrats process papers at a high rate of speed. It is often frustrating to attempt to merge two New York corporations because the personnel in the secretary of state's office get around to clearing the paperwork only in their own sweet time. Further, Delaware maintains a separate court system—the Court of Chancery—to adjudicate (without the nuisance, for corporate practitioners anyway, of jury trials) issues involving the structure and governance of domestic corporations. Moreover, a modern statute such as Delaware's is generally permissive; the glitches which can frustrate counsel attempting to close on a financing have been ironed out.

Further, law firms around the country are willing to give opinions on matters involving Delaware law because of the general familiarity of the corporate bar with the Delaware statute and the cases interpreting it. The ability of counsel to opine on an issue is no trivial matter. Without the requisite opinion of counsel, no public stock offering or merger will go forward. Loan agreements routinely require comfort from the company's counsel in the form of opinions. Incorporating in Delaware gives the founder assurances that counsel will be able to render and/or appraise the necessary opinions to underwriters, lenders, merger partners, and others to enable business aims to be accomplished.

The foregoing is not designed as an uncritical hymn of praise in favor of Delaware incorporation. Other states are conforming to advanced notions of corporate practice and some—for example, Maryland in the area of franchise taxes—are actually to be preferred on some issues. However, Delaware is the rod against which other possibilities should be measured.

chapter six

Tax Discussion for the Nonlawyer: Minimizing Taxes in the Early Stages

Tax considerations play a crucial part in the elections made upon the commencement of a start-up business. Tax concerns are ubiquitous in any financial environment, but mistakes made upon initial organization often cannot be remedied adequately; the opportunities are forever lost.

For purposes of this discussion, it is assumed that the corporate form has been elected. To understand fully the intricacies of those provisions of the Internal Revenue Code impacting various aspects of corporate organization, one must appreciate that the federal government does not impose a wealth tax on individuals' intangible assets. State and local jurisdictions tax property—real and personal—on an annual basis, and both the federal and state governments levy an ad valorem tax (measured by the value of the asset) on the estates of well-off decedents. However, at the federal level and in most states, paper wealth—cash and securities—is not subject to an annual tax on dormant value, and increases in an individual's wealth, without more, are not subject to a transaction tax while he is alive. Governments are not, however, sleepy. They want to take a portion of the individuals' increases in wealth—to share in their good fortune so to speak—but the governments have generally restricted themselves to assessing tax only upon the occurrence of certain events. It is thought easier to establish the amount of the increase, and therefore tax it, by focusing on transfers: the passage of assets from one hand, or form, to another. In organizing a corporation, therefore, the first rule is to circumvent taxable events: transfers which the Code (and state law) recognize as an occasion for asserting a tax. If a taxable event is unavoidable, the second rule is to eliminate or avoid gain if possible and, if not, to defer the recognition of such gain or, if the circumstances so warrant, to establish a loss.

Incorporation involves several transfers which might occasion tax. Thus, the organizing corporation typically issues stock in exchange for cash, property, or in some cases, expressly for services. The issuance of equity securities does not create income to the corporation. On the other hand, the recipient of the stock is, potentially at least, taxed on any gain resulting from the exchange. However, the recipient usually avoids tax, for a variety of reasons. Thus, payment for shares in cash, and only in cash, does not trigger a tax because no gain is recognized when one pays cash; the taxpayer's "basis" for tax purposes in cash is always equal to the cash paid. Similarly, the receipt of stock worth $100 for property with a tax "basis" ("basis" being a term of art with a structured meaning in the tax law, generally equating to "investment") of $100 does not involve gain or loss. The possibility of exposure occurs, therefore, upon the issuance of stock: (1) in exchange for appreciated property; and/or (2) in payment for past or future services (in those states where such services are eligible consideration for stock issuance), including occasions upon which the IRS recharacterizes a stock-for-property transaction as in fact stock for services.

Section 351 postpones gain or loss on the contribution of appreciated property to a corporation in exchange for stock, assuming certain rules are followed. Note that, although §351 is thought of principally in connection with organization of unseasoned start-ups, in fact the issuer can be newly organized or pre-existing when the stock issuance occurs; it can be any size, have an unlimited number of shareholders pre- and postfinancing, and issue as many classes of stock as the situation warrants. The principle of postponing tax is not dependent on the resultant corporation being small or uncomplicated. The rule of §351 is that, immediately after the financing, the investors who contribute property and/or cash in exchange for stock in the transaction are in control; that is, they own at least 80 percent of the issuer's combined voting power (all classes of voting stock) and 80 percent of each class of nonvoting stock. If such is the case (and the property is not subject to liabilities in excess of its basis), no gain will be recognized on any appreciated property so transferred. And, according to the usual rules governing tax-postponed transactions, the tax basis of that property in the hands of the corporation will be "carried over" from the basis of the contributor, adjusted (increased) for any gain recognized by the contributor.

Note some of the things §351 *does not* do. It does not solve the "cheap stock" problem: when a founder, employee, consultant, and others are receiving stock in exchange for past or future services and want to avoid tax. In fact, if one of the stock buyers is paying solely in services and only services (past or future) and getting back more than 20 percent of the issuer's voting power, the entire transaction will be disqualified, much to the distress of the individual(s) in the buying syndicate putting up appreciated property.

The more significant question is implicit in the foregoing discussion. When is the founder's secret process "property" for purposes of §351 and when is it "services," occasioning tax to the founder and perhaps to other contributors of property relying on §351 to shield their gain? The distinction is, again, a little bit like the opposing nature of light—both a particle and a wave at the same time; a secret process is "property"—it has an owner and can be sold, *and* it is a reflection, a result, of past services, of capitalized labor. As Shakespeare has suggested, nomenclature is significant. Leaving literature in favor of the mundane provisions of the Code, Revenue Procedure 69-19 sets out the basic guidelines. Summarizing that complex document, the information should be legally protectible (i.e., at least a trade secret), and in fact adequate safeguards taken to guard the secret, "original, unique, and novel" (though not necessarily patentable) and not "developed especially [sic]" for the transferee. The information should not represent mere knowledge or efficiency resulting from skill or experience. It is helpful in this regard if any future services to be rendered by the transferee to the issuer respecting the process are bought and paid for under a separate contract negotiated at arm's length.

CHEAP STOCK TO EMPLOYEES AND PROMOTERS:
THE "EAT-'EM-ALL-UP" PREFERRED STOCK APPROACH

Again to state a fundamental proposition, there is no available cash in an early-stage financing with which to pay federal and/or state income taxes. Consequently, anything that smacks of a taxable event is verboten. The norm, however, is that the founders will obtain their interests in the new entity in consideration of past services and/or the capitalized value of the founders' talents and services to be rendered; the promoters, if different from the founders, are obtaining stock for their organizational efforts. The omnipresent danger is that the IRS will successfully assert the position that all or a portion of the stock issued to the founders has been, for tax purposes, issued for services and a current tax is payable. Since that position reflects the economic reality, it is dangerous.

There are, however, three principal weapons on the side of the tax-payer. First, as indicated, §351 of the Code provides for nonrecognition of gain or loss upon the exchange of property for shares if the shareholders contributing cash or property are in "control" (meaning ownership of 80 percent of the stock) of the corporation after the transaction. The trick, within the bounds of reasonableness and good faith, is to argue that the founder's contribution is not "services," but intangible property—that is, a secret process or other proprietary information—because secret processes can be "property" under the Code. The second, the "passage-of-time" approach, is described below.

Thirdly, if the consideration paid by the founder cannot in good conscience be labeled "property," and the investors all come in together, then the inquiry turns to the value of the stock being issued. Assume the founder pays, as he always can, some small amount of cash. Is that cash sufficient to equal the "value" of the stock received so that no gain is recognizable? At first blush, if the founder pays $10 per share and the investors contemporaneously pay $100 per share, it looks as if the founder has made a bargain purchase and an element of taxable compensation has changed hands. However, the compensatory element may disappear if the investors receive preferred stock. The Internal Revenue Service has never challenged successfully the view that the issuance of shares with a liquidation preference—ordinarily labeled "preferred stock"—can "eat up" value in an amount equal to the preference, thereby reducing the common stock (the "cheap stock") to marginal value. Put another way, if the liquidation preference of the preferred stock is equal to the cash contributions of the parties contributing cash capital, then a balance-sheet test immediately after organization suggests that the common stock is "worth" only the nominal consideration the founders have paid, thereby excluding any element that can be attributed to past or future services. See the following, a hypothetical balance sheet.

Balance Sheet

Assets		Liabilities	
Cash	$10,000		-0-
		Shareholders' Equity *Preferred Stock* *(1,000 shares)* *outstanding,* *$10 par, convertible* *into 1,000 shares of* *common stock*	$10,000
		Common Stock *(1,000 shares)* *outstanding,* *10¢ par*	100
	$10,000		$10,100

An uncritical examination of the balance sheet might suggest that 10¢ a share paid by the common would compare equitably—that is, no bargain purchase—with the $10 paid by the preferred, since the preferred appears superior to the common on the balance sheet in the full amount of the cash paid. Certainly, if the issuer were liquidated immediately after it was formed—that is, on the date the taxable event, if any, occurred—the common shareholders would get back just what they put in, $100. Of course, since no one intends to liquidate the corporation either right away, or, for that matter, ever (and, indeed, if it is liquidated, it is unlikely that either the common or the preferred will get anything), the liquidation value test is dependent on a contrary-to-fact convention, but nonetheless a convention that has stood the test of time in view of what appears to be the silent acquiescence of the Internal Revenue Service.

The power of the preferred to "eat up" value for tax purposes is enhanced to the extent the preferred shareholder owns additional superior rights, that is, senior as to dividends (of which there are usually none), special voting rights, registration rights, and the like. These rights are often significant to the cash investors in the early going and are helpful on the tax issue; from the founder's point of view, the fact that they fade away upon the exit date—the IPO, for example, means he can be relatively indifferent. It could, of course, be argued that one must weight the common's value upwards because all the "upside" belongs to the common; however, making the preferred convertible, albeit at a price of $10 per share, means that the preferred has a chance to share in the "upside" as well. In short, ordinarily the cash investors take convertible preferred shares (a choice which, parenthetically, excludes an election of S Corporation status), and the founder, common.

The principal caveat has to do with excess. In the example quoted, the cash investor's payment per share is 100 times the amount of the founder's payment. Many practitioners are uncomfortable with a spread that great. Others tend to take the more aggressive view. The belt-and-suspenders technique is to combine the "eat-'em-all-up" preferred approach with the "passage-of-time," or "Bruce Berckmans," approach discussed immediately below.

As indicated, it can be important to contributing shareholders other than the founder that the "eat-'em-all-up" approach works. To be sure, the biggest risk is to the taxpayer held to have received stock for services. However, any shareholder contributing appreciated property may be required to pay tax if the taxpayer deemed to have contributed services gets more than 20 percent of the resultant stock, since, as stated, §351 only works if the contributors of cash and property, not services, get 80 percent or more of the stock.

STOCK FOR SERVICES:
THE "PASSAGE-OF-TIME" APPROACH

The complementary device for allocating the founder his cheap stock tax free involves organizing the start-up entity as soon as the founder starts to consider a maiden voyage. To the extent the founder receives his shares well prior to the first-round financing, the founder/taxpayer can argue that the passage of time and events accounts for the increase in value—$10 for the investors' stock versus 10¢ for his shares. The risk is that the IRS will successfully argue "step transaction." However, that argument is vitiated if the financing was only a contingency when the founder's stock was issued, the moral of the story being that it usually does not cost anything to organize the start-up as early as possible and may provide substantial tax comfort.

The lesson, in sum, signaled by the discussion in this and the previous section is that the early bird catches the worm. Once the first round of financing has occurred, the dimension of the "cheap-stock" issue changes. It is considerably dicier to contend that the preferred "eats up" value when common shares have traded in the interim or otherwise been priced in arm's-length transactions. The planning process must shift to the arena of executive compensation, that is, stock equivalents, stock options, restricted stock bought with borrowed company funds, and so forth. (The importance of the question whether the employee shares are issued at less than fair-market value is not confined to the tax arena. Bargain stock will create compensation expense on the company's books, impacting earnings as the discussion in chapter 11 points out in greater detail.)

SECTION 83 AND STOCK SUBJECT TO VESTING

Section 83(a) of the Internal Revenue Code states that if "property" is issued "in connection with the performance of services," the difference between the "fair value" of, and the amount paid by the recipient for, the property—usually stock— is taxable to the recipient (and deductible by the corporation) as additional compensation as of the earlier of: (1) the first date forfeiture restraints (if any) lapse, or (2) the first date the property is transferable, value being calculated without regard to restrictions other than those which by their terms never lapse. If an employee is buying stock at a bargain and there are no "substantial" forfeiture risks (other than those which will never lapse) attached, then the impact of §83 is relatively simple—the recipient pays tax on the bargain element upon receipt of the stock.

Section 83 becomes of cardinal importance in venture financings in which employees are acquiring "restricted" stock, meaning stock subject to contractual restraints on transferability and risks of "forfeiture." Despite the fact that restricted stock (in the sense of nonvested stock) can be issued at any time during a corporation's lifetime, the issue is discussed in this chapter, since it routinely arises on corporate organization.

The purpose of vesting restrictions is to tie footloose employees to the corporation with "golden handcuffs." Typically, an employee will be allowed to purchase at bargain prices shares of stock subject to the company's right to buy them back at the employee's nominal cost if the employee prematurely terminates his employment for reasons other than death or disability. Thus, a five-year vesting restriction will typically provide that one-fifth of the shares issued shall vest in each of the five years following the employee's receipt of stock; that is, they are no longer repurchasable by the corporation at cost. The vesting constraint goes hand in hand with an absolute, albeit limited in time, restraint on alienation; the employee cannot dispose of shares to anyone until they are vested. Without that constraint (unless it is clear the forfeiture restriction is binding on transferees, in which case no one would buy at any sensible price), the forfeiture restriction would have little economic bite. If the employee were originally issued 1,000 shares and left of his own accord in the third year following the employee's receipt of stock, the employee would own 400 shares outright and 600 shares would be repurchasable at the employee's cost.

Under §83(a), an employee "lucking" into the opportunity to buy restricted, nonvested stock at a bargain has a problem. He receives a piece of paper he cannot readily sell; and he incurs a contingent liability to pay at some later date tax on the difference between his nominal cost and the artificial "value" of that security, as at a future time. For purposes of computing the tax, such value is calculated as if, contrary to fact, the employee could sell the shares into an auction market, since "investment-letter" restrictions do not count in computing value. Arguably, therefore, the receipt of nonvested stock is no bargain, because when the tax becomes payable (i.e., the forfeiture risk lapses), the stock may be (indeed it is expected to be) highly "valuable" and the tax burdens accordingly aggravated. The potential "Catch-22" is apparent: A owes tax on a $10 stock which he cannot sell—perhaps at any price—and has no way of realizing the cash with which to pay the tax; he pays out of other assets and holds, expecting an IPO which never materializes, and his stock eventually becomes worthless.

The answer to the predicament lies in the provisions of §83(b). As long as value can be measured when the shares are initially issued, the tax problem is not calamitous because the employee is receiving stock at a time when its value, however calculated, is low. Thus, if the early-round cash investors are coming in at $1 per share and the employee is paying 60¢ a share, at least the amount of the tax is calculable: 40¢ times the number of shares sold, times the employee's effective rate of federal tax. (Indeed, if the cash investors buy preferred stock, then the employee may claim no tax is due.) And, the privilege afforded by §83(b) is that the taxpayer may make an election; that is, he may file, within thirty days after the stock has been originally purchased, notice of his choice to pay tax on the difference between the value of the stock received at that time and the amount actually paid for the stock. Once that tax is paid, then vesting restrictions become irrelevant. The stock may go to $100 per share when the employee finally vests with respect to the last share, but no taxable event will occur.

The §83(b) election also changes the nature of the income. If the election is made, then the subsequent tax event occurs upon the sale of stock, and any gain at that time is capital gain. In the absence of the election, the tax event occurs upon vesting and the character upon vesting will be ordinary income. Only the post-vesting appreciation will be capital gain.

It is important to keep in mind that the §83(b) election is available and should be made, even though the employee purchases shares at full value at the time of issuance. It is not, in other words, the fact that the employee is purchasing cheap stock, but that he's purchasing stock *subject to a risk of forfeiture*, which casts the taxable event out into the future; it's usually true that such stock is cheap stock, otherwise why would anyone agree to the forfeiture restrictions, but such need not always be the case. The virtue of the §83(b) election is that it pulls that event back to the present day, when the gap between the employee's payment and the value of the stock is presumably at its narrowest.

The §83(b) election is not without its risks. If the property declines in value, then the loss would be a capital loss. Under such circumstances and in the absence of the election, the compensatory element would be reduced or disappear. Thus if A receives stock worth $1,000 for free, the §83(b) election results in $1,000 of ordinary income. If the stock declines in value to $400 when A vests and immediately sells the stock, A would have a $600 capital loss. In the absence of the election, A would only have $400 of ordinary income upon vesting.

chapter seven

Drafting the Business Plan and the Placement Memo

Since a private placement memorandum, usually abbreviated as the PPM, is the norm in most deals, the founder should familiarize himself with the standards for memorandum preparation, keeping in mind that, like any legal document, there are various audiences. The audience composed of potential plaintiffs (and, theoretically at least, the SEC enforcement staff) will read the document against the requirements contained in the cases imposing liability. The audience composed of investors will read the document for its substantive content: "What are the terms of the deal?" To professional investors interested enough to become potential buyers, the private placement memorandum is a handy collection of only some of the information they are interested in, plus a lot of surplus verbiage (the empty language about suitability standards, for example). To the issuer, it is a sales document, putting the best face possible on the company and its prospects. To the managers, the memorandum is a summary of the business plan. Indeed, it may incorporate the business plan as an exhibit or be "wrapped around" the plan itself—a memorialization of how the business is to be conducted.

The first page of the PPM, the cover page, contains some of the information one might see on the front of a statutory prospectus: name of the issuer, summary description of the securities to be sold, whether the issue is primary (proceeds to the issuer) and/or secondary (proceeds to selling shareholders), the price per share, the gross and net proceeds (minus selling commissions and expenses), and a risk factor or two (that is, the offering is "highly speculative" and the securities will not be liquid). Some would argue a date is important, because, legally, the document speaks as of a certain date. However, if the memo becomes substantively stale between the offer and the closing, it is critical that the issuer update and circulate it; omission of material information as of the closing is not excusable on the theory that the memo displays an earlier date. Moreover, a dated memorandum will appear just that— dated—if a few months elapse and the issue is still unsold. A related issue is whether to specify a minimum amount of proceeds which must be subscribed if the offering is to go forward. If the financing is subject to a "minimum," a reference belongs on the cover page. It makes common sense that there be a critical mass in most placements; however, a *stated* requirement that X dollars be raised or all subscriptions returned inhibits an early-closing strategy—the ability to "close," if only in escrow—with the most eager of the issuer's potential investors. Such "closings" may not be substantively meaningful; the deal may be that the "closing" will be revisited if more money is not raised. However, a first closing can have a salubrious shock effect on the overall financing; it can bring to a halt ongoing (sometimes interminable) negotiations on the terms of the deal and create a bandwagon effect.

The cover page should be notated, a handwritten number inscribed to help record the destination of each private placement memorandum. It is also customary to reflect self-serving, exculpatory language (of varying effectiveness in protecting the issuer), that is:

1. The offer is only an offer in jurisdictions where it can be legally made and then only to persons meeting suitability standards imposed by state and federal law. (The offer is, in fact, an "offer" whenever and to whomsoever a court designates.)

2. The memorandum is not to be reproduced (about the same effectiveness as stamping Department of Defense papers "Eyes Only," a legend understood in bureaucratese to mean, "may be important . . . make several copies").

3. No person is authorized to give out any information other than that contained in the memo. (Since the frequent practice is for selling

agents to expand liberally on the memo's contents, it would be extraordinary if extraneous statements by an authorized agent of the issuer were not allowed in evidence against the issuer, unless perhaps they are expressly inconsistent with the language of the memo.)

4. The private placement memorandum contains summaries of important documents (a statement of the obvious), and the summaries are "qualified by reference" to the full documentation. (A materially inaccurate summary is unlikely to be excused simply because investors were cautioned to read the entire instrument.)

5. Each investor is urged to consult his own attorney and accountant. (No one knows what this means; if the legally expertise portions of the private placement memorandum are otherwise actionably false, it would take an unusually forgiving judge to decide the plaintiff should have obeyed the command and hired personal counsel.)

6. The offering has not been registered under the '33 Act and the SEC has not approved it.

The foregoing is not meant as an exercise in fine legal writing and the avoidance of excess verbiage. Certain legends are mandatory as a matter of good lawyering—a summary of the "risk factors"; a statement that investors may ask questions and review answers and obtain additional information (an imperative of Reg. D); and, of course, the language required by various state securities administrators. A recitation tipping investors that they will be required in the subscription documents to make representations about their wealth and experience is generally desirable, particularly in light of cases finding against plaintiffs who falsified their representation. However, in my opinion, a cover page loaded with superfluous exculpations may cheapen a venture financing, signaling to readers that the deal is borderline, in a league with "double write-off" offerings in the real estate and tax-shelter areas.

A well-written private placement memorandum will follow the cover page with a summary of the offering. This section corresponds to a term sheet, except that the language is usually spelled out, not abbreviated. The important points are covered briefly: a description of the terms of the offering, the company's business, risk factors, additional terms (i.e., antidilution protection, registration rights, control features), expenses of the transaction and summary financial information. The purpose of the summary is to make the offering easy to read and understand. As stated, suppliers of capital are inundated with business plans and private placement memoranda; the sales-conscious issuer must get all the salient facts in as conspicuous a position as possible if he hopes to have them noticed.

At this juncture, it is customary to reproduce investor suitability standards, identifying and flagging the principal requirements for a Reg. D offering, that is, the definition of "accredited investor."

Issuers should approach offerings that have stated maximums and minimums with caution. The SEC has made its position clear. If the issuer elects to increase or decrease the size of the offering above the stated maximum/minimum, each of the investors who have signed subscription agreements must consent to the change in writing. It is *not* open to the issuer to send out a notice to the effect that "We are raising or lowering the minimum and, if we do not hear from you, we assume you consent." The issuer must obtain the affirmative consent of each investor, which may be a bit difficult if the investor is, at that point, somewhere in Katmandu.

Investors should be aware that issuers sometimes do not want the investors to know certain information. For example, some issuers elect to code the numbers on the private placement memorandum so that no investor knows he is receiving, say, number 140; he is, instead, receiving "14-G."

Parenthetically, if counsel to the issuer are careful, one sentence the memorandum *will not* contain is the name of the issuer's counsel; if named, the law firm involved may be assuming responsibilities to the purchasers of the securities.

Risk Factors

For maximum caveat-emptor value, the "risk factors" section should be referenced on the first page and reproduced in full in a position in the memo prior to the sections in which the attractiveness of the opportunity is trumpeted. Several recitations are standard, indeed would be conspicuous by their absence, namely:

1. The company is in its "development"—that is, most highly vulnerable—stage; its products haven't been proven or marketed.

2. Its success is highly dependent on a few key individuals, none of whom have run a company of any size before.

3. There are fearsome competitors on the horizon.

4. The company will need more than one round of financing to survive.

5. The securities are illiquid.

6. Substantial "dilution" is involved.

7. A few major customers form the backbone of the order bank.

8. The technology is not entirely (or at all) protected by patents or copyrights.

These should be fleshed out with risks specific to the issue: environmental problems, the possibility of technical obsolescence, difficulties in procuring drug licenses from the FDA, and so forth.

The importance of the risk factors cannot be emphasized too strongly. A recent federal statute (actually one law in 1995 and a second in 1998 to close a loophole) immunize the sponsors from suit if their "forward-looking statements" are accompanied by "meaningful" cautions. Moreover, significant recent cases have upheld (albeit not yet at the Supreme Court level) the bulletproofing effect of language which "bespeaks caution" in a disclosure document, bulletproof in this case meaning a document on which may be founded a successful motion for disposing of a complaint on the pleadings and prior to trial. Courts have, of late, been niggardly in allowing claims to proceed based on "forward-looking" statements which turn out to be inaccurate—claims of "fraud by hindsight" as Judge Friendly has put it—provided there is prominent disclosure of the risks. The decisions have involved both public and private offerings. The defense, however, is not absolute, particularly in light of the Supreme Court's dictum in *Virginia Bankshares* that "not every mixture with the true will neutralize the deceptions." As one commentator has put it:

> Drafting good risk factors takes time, effort and creativity, since they cannot generally be taken from a standard form or borrowed from disclosures made by another registrant. The effort of crafting well-tailored risk factors is rewarded, however, not only by better risk factors disclosure but also by improved insight into the business of the registrant. Such insight can favorably impact the quality of the disclosure in the prospectus or report as a whole.

Some practitioners take the view that covering risks once in the risk-factors section satisfies the registrant's disclosure obligation fully. A more conservative view is that risk factors are primarily excerpts from the disclosure document and that each risk, or at least each of the most significant ones, should also be discussed elsewhere in the document.

On occasion, the founder will argue with counsel that a given risk factor is stated too negatively. In this author's view, that argument is generally a waste of time. Few sophisticated investors are influenced by the risk-factors section. They form their independent judgment on the issues; its utility is more prophylactic than educational.

Following the risk-factors section, the private placement memorandum should set out the terms (previously summarized) of the deal;

that is, the special features of the securities being offered (preferences, voting rights, conversion privilege, dividends, and so forth), the pricing terms (payable all at one time or in installments), and what the placement agent is being paid. Many private placement memoranda do not include in either the summary or the early discussion an up-front disclosure of the expenses of the transaction, particularly the legal fees. That information usually can be extruded from the pro forma financials, but nondisclosure is not recommended—even though embarrassingly high placement and legal fees may mean to the experienced reader that the offer is sticky and has been "out on the street" for a while.

At or about this point, an SEC regulation requires a *public* prospectus to discuss the use to which proceeds of the offering are to be put. However, unless the issuer plans to pay down debt or use any such proceeds for the benefit of an insider (in which case the discussion should be quite specific), the initial draft of this language is usually cryptic and stylized—"working capital" or "general corporate purposes"—partly out of a desire to avoid leaking sensitive information. To be sure, once negotiations begin, the "use of proceeds" is often a heavily negotiated item. The investors often want a concrete menu, in part to meet the problem discussed earlier, when the start-up has too much money. However, their policing mechanism is not necessarily a sharpened description in the private placement memorandum. The more usual provision is a promise in the Stock Purchase Agreement, tied either to a specific schedule or to the effect that expenditures over, say, $25,000 are subject to an advance approval process.

One of the most widely read segments of the memo is the discussion of management, the curricula vitae of the directors and senior officers, together with an exposition of their compensation. In the start-up world, nothing is tranquil. Thus, in describing the management team even the disclosure of names may on occasion be dicey; some people will agree to join the officer corps of a start-up if and only if the financing is successful. It is permissible, because there is no other solution, to denote these individuals as Doctor X and Mister Y. Disclosure of compensation dollars can also be sensitive, but the requirements of the SEC for public offerings are sufficiently specific to indicate the Commission means business. Prudent issuers should fully set forth for all senior employees the terms of the employment agreement, any understandings concerning bonuses, the "parachutes" (i.e., the penalty paid if the employee is dismissed), and the stock arrangements. The investors are likely to zero in on the agreements between the firm and its key managers; the memo should disclose how the managers have had their wagons hitched to the company with noncompete clauses and "golden handcuffs."

There is a relatively high potential for embarrassment in this section for those charged with due diligence. For some perverse reason, resumés often contain easily checkable lies (*X* claims a doctorate in chemical engineering from Purdue when he didn't complete the course). Moreover, federal and state laws contain so-called "bad boy" provisions, meaning that disclosures are required and exemptions from registration are not available if anyone connected with the issue (or the issuer) has in the recent past been convicted of crimes or subjected to administrative proceedings which are relevant to the sale of securities. An overlooked felony conviction for mail fraud (particularly if a computer search on the Nexis system would have disclosed it) can be more embarrassing than a phony degree.

CERTAIN TRANSACTIONS

The compensation issue overlaps with a section on conflicts of interest. This section, mandated by rule in public offerings and by prudence in private placements, requires the disclosure of any transactions between the issuer and its insiders, the company leasing its offices from the founder, for example. Tax implications lurk below the surface; if goods or services are exchanged with an employee at bargain prices, the bargain element may be considered compensation. Corporate law also imposes a gloss. Insider transactions may be avoided later as a result of a lawsuit by a disgruntled stockholder unless the transaction is approved by disinterested directors and/or stockholders or is "fair" to the corporation. The institution of a financing, public or private, often is the occasion for reviewing and canceling some of those "sweetheart" deals. The disclosure requirement can be therapeutic and educational, educating the founder on what it means to have partners.

The level of diligence required in presenting the facts in a private placement is not as well fleshed out in the cases and authorities as in the case of a public offering. A defective-disclosure document in a public offering is scrutinized against the background of §11 of the '33 Act, where liability for misstatements can be close to absolute. The principal federal provision governing private placements is found in Rule 10b-5, promulgated under the '34 Act, which talks in terms of fraud and deceit and thus has been held to require proof of some form of *scienter*, a legal term entailing knowing violations of the appropriate standard. The sections of the securities laws governing liability for faulty disclosure in nonregistered offerings, state and federal, vary in the standards of diligence required, but the burden is less than the duty of active investigation imposed by §11.

In the final analysis, the private placement memorandum is a compromise document, entailing a trade-off between the durability of a bulletproof statutory prospectus versus the expense entailed in preparing such a presentation to investors. Founders and their advisers have to face the problem squarely. If the financing involves no more than, say, $750,000, there is a line which counsel cannot cross in spending time drafting the private placement memorandum. A business plan coupled with prudential caveats—for example, the risk factors—may be the best anyone can do in the circumstances. The trade-off issue should not be read to suggest the problem of antifraud liability is insignificant. Many of the built-in comforts and safeguards for the issuer in a public offering—the SEC staff's letter of comment, the use of Regulation S-K as a guide, the existence of audited financial statements, and other expertised portions of the registration statement—are not available in a private placement. Moreover, even the lawyers keep their heads below the lip of the trench; most law firms take the view that issuers and placement agents are not entitled to an opinion that a private placement does not violate the antifraud provisions of the securities laws.

Prudence suggests that each purchaser be required to fill out and file with the issuer documents in aid of the issuer's ability to claim an exemption from the requirement that the securities be registered under federal and state law. The statements made by the purchaser also serve to stop him from claiming he was deceived in the course of the offering. The inclination of issuers—and it appears to be sound— is to load up the subscription documents with a combination of exculpatory language, concessions by the investor as to his status as a "smart and rich" investor (see below) and representations that he has in fact done the sort of things (i.e., read the memo, consulted his own advisers) the private placement memorandum urges him to do. In light of the few cases of any relevance, there does not appear to be harm in going overboard, despite the fact that investors routinely sign the subscription agreement and questionnaire without reading them and the language is rarely an item for negotiation.

BUSINESS PLAN

The heart of the document is the description of the business. Some practitioners like to draft this section afresh, as if a prospectus were being prepared. The contrary, and I believe the better, view is that the issuer's business plan should be incorporated more or less verbatim into the private placement memorandum by attaching it as an exhibit and/or excerpting passages into a "wrap-around" or "sandwich" memo. The business plan is the meat inside the standard disclosures. The argument in favor of rewriting the business plan in legalese is that the plan may be overly optimistic, and, therefore, should be sanitized before its thrust is incorporated into a disclosure document. The counterargument is that, if the case comes to trial, witnesses for the issuer may spend days on the stand under hostile cross-examination, lamely attempting to explain differences between the document that was produced for investor scrutiny and the one that management used for its own purposes.

The business plan for an early-stage investment opportunity is traditionally drafted by or at the supervision of the founder because there is little room in early-stage financings for investment bankers. If the venture opportunity is mezzanine stage, then the business plan may be reviewed by investment bankers advising the seller, the investors, or both. In either event, the business plan is the foundation for the private placement memorandum, or "book" as it is often called, and accordingly it deserves comment.

There is a copious amount of material on how to draft business plans that will attract interest in the investment community. Of course, every business is different. The organization of a plan that makes good sense for one enterprise may be wholly inappropriate for another. However, there is a consensus on the key elements that should be discussed if the plan is to compete with others in the capital markets. And, one way to understand those key elements is to examine the table of contents of someone else's plan or, better, a composite of a number of plans. Such a composite is Section 2.10, prepared by Paul Brountas, one of the most experienced lawyers in the venture-capital business. It is set forth at the end of the chapter and is a useful guide against which to check one's own efforts, if only to see what is being left out. The following discussion will not attempt to comment on each item set forth in the composite table. Rather, areas of unusual interest which deserve special attention are highlighted in the following discussion.

The Marketing Section: The Single-Most Important Section for Early-Stage Investments

As earlier indicated, the marketing section is the most troublesome for many founders to write convincingly and should, in view of the significance venture investors pay to the issue, be the most carefully drafted. It is relatively easy to obtain industry statistics and divide by some number. For example:

> The overall market for product X is \$1.5 billion per year and we plan to capture, "conservatively," 10 percent, which means we project \$150 million in annual sales. Our strategy is to pursue the following niches. . . .

All the words are appealing and familiar; venture capitalists are expected to applaud a niche strategy, meaning that the approach to the market is focused on an area where competition will be minimal and a substantial market share is ripe for the plucking. The term "conservative" is also routinely joined to an entrepreneur's forecast. However, a well-done plan does not stop there—a number of questions remain to be answered. For example, what determines the niche? Price? (Few successful venture strategies are driven by the idea of being the lowest-cost producer.) Quality? Performance? Geography? Service? Proprietary information? Is the market growing? How will competitors (presumably larger and better financed) be kept at bay? How will the market be penetrated? Will the issuer train its own sales force, use manufacturers' representatives, joint venture with another supplier or vendor? Will it advertise? What are the promotional plans? Direct mail? Trade shows? What service and warranty policies will be followed?

One critical feature for many sophisticated investors is evidence that the marketing section has been drafted and then subjected to multiple revisions, that the plan has been gone over a number of times by persons bringing varying backgrounds and experience to the issue. Many a venture capitalist will be delighted to find a candid confession that the overall business strategy actually changed after an in-the-field investigation of market potential.

Indeed, the more specificity the better. Thus, a sophisticated marketing plan will designate the magazines and other media outlets in which the firm plans to advertise, and identify the trade shows, the territories a sales office can be expected to cover, perhaps even provide proposed ratios, such as the expected ratio of successful sales per sales calls.

The coda to the marketing section, either made a part of it or placed in the immediate vicinity, is the section on competition. One experienced investor representative starts each discussion with a founder by asking for a discourse on competition; if the founder has not thought the issue through, the interview is rapidly brought to a close. Investors are generally unwilling to believe that, even with the most impregnable protection for proprietary information, competition can be kept at bay for very long. It is essential, therefore, to zero in on the existing (and likely future) competition and indicate as specifically as possible why and how the new entrant will be able to steal a march on the other firms, what legal and economic obstacles can be strewn in their path, how long the monopoly will last, and so forth.

Business Strategy and
the Single-Product Problem

Many start-up companies, organized around what the founder believes is an earthshaking item of "science," are puzzled and upset when venture investors turn the cold shoulder. Often, the problem is that the investors perceive the company as lacking a long-range strategy, incapable of producing more than the single product then on the drawing board or in production; that capability is generally viewed as too limited by the professional investment community. A successful business plan, at least for a technologically oriented start-up, should admit that high-tech companies cannot survive solely by selling their current products, no matter how advanced and revolutionary. They must sell as well an intangible—the belief that they will be able to offer future sophisticated and reliable products so that the customer will be assured of a stable and reliable vendor who will always provide state-of-the-art products at competitive prices. The "value" purchased by investors and customers alike is, in large part, the capacity of the company to follow today's "great products" with unlimited future "great products." The business plan should, accordingly, explore at some length how the company is going to grow into long pants, the strategies for expanding markets and product lines once the initial products have been successfully marketed.

Management

Of vast importance is the quality of management, the venture investor's rubric being to "bet the jockey, not the horse." In addition to describing current team members, the business plan should discuss how and when new members will be added, how the management team will be compensated, and how the team members will be motivated to perform to maximize the objectives of the business as laid out in the plan. It is not easy to recruit experienced-quality people for a new venture; romance or no romance, school tuitions are a source of concern. If the management team is skeletal, investors may be cynical, recalling the old saw that recruitment takes one month for each $10,000 in salary; that is, it takes nine months to recruit a $90,000-a-year marketing manager.

Beefing up the Board of Directors

Locating useful directors for a start-up company is difficult but often vital. While the founder, his wife, and his lawyer comprise the paradigmatic start-up board, perceptive organizers try to fill gaps in their business expertise by adding experienced directors. Start-ups backed by professionally managed venture firms are lucky: the investors' representative ordinarily makes an enormous contribution. Many emerging companies do not enjoy professional backing in the first round. Accordingly, with no money to pay for full- or part-time experts, a founder is often well-advised to dangle directorships, coupled with cheap stock, in front of experienced individual businessmen. In today's corporate world, as multinationals change ownership relentlessly and fashion dictates that white-collar staffs be pared to the bone, a large cohort of relatively young, dynamic, and highly competent businesspeople have been released into the workforce. Many are loath to return to the large corporate environment; they are disgusted and enraged at the big-company culture, and they have "parachutes" which relieve them of the necessity of working full time. Thus they are prime candidates to help nurture an emerging business to maturity. Accordingly, it is becoming increasingly an integral part of an advanced venture strategy to harness the energy of early retirees, inducing them to join start-up boards and fill in the experience gap.

There are subtle issues to be resolved in pursuing this strategy, however. To be sure, the engagement of an experienced businessperson to sit in a key board seat may, indeed, provide a greater degree of "hands-on" oversight than can be expected from a harassed, overworked young partner in a venture-capital pool; often the fledgling venture manager's advice can grate on the founder's ears, particularly if the board member's prior experience is limited to attending classes at the Harvard Business School. However, it may be equally troublesome for the founder to take advice from someone other than the person who put up the money, particularly a refugee from a big-company culture. A venture manager may lose vital impact and feel for a portfolio company if his advice is filtered through a retiree whose stake in the company is limited to the upside on his options. When a partner in the investment firm takes a position, his hide is on the line. He made the investment, and the founder may be more inclined to view him as entitled to lay down the law.

OTHER ISSUES

The plan should, of course, articulate the exit strategy, explaining how the venture proposes to get to the point where it can cash out the investors. A carefully prepared business plan will usually contain third-party endorsements, ranging from letters from satisfied customers, to studies by independent consultants, to a "cold comfort" or "negative assurance" letter from public accountants concerning the projections.

The writer should organize his topics, particularly the executive summary, with the understanding that investors are extraordinarily busy and will skim the document. Brevity is thus critical. Indeed, one expert suggests the plan be prepared assuming the reader will only devote five minutes to it, attempting in that period to accomplish the following:

- Determine the characteristics of the company and the industry;

- Determine the terms of the deal;

- Read the latest balance sheet;

- Determine the caliber of the people in the deal;

- Determine what is different about this deal;

- Give the plan a once-over-lightly.

In terms of quick "turn-ons," additional attractions to investors include the following: hard evidence that the managers plan to "focus," another way of saying that a target market has been thoroughly researched and identified; testimonials (if possible) from actual or potential customers, validating in checkable form the marketing assumptions; and a documented story on proprietary protection of intellectual property, including not just a reference to, but a discussion of, existing or pending patents and the trade-secret protection program.

PROJECTIONS—THE "BULL'S-EYE" THEORY OF FORECASTING: "SHOOT HIGH"

The art of preparing forecasts in a business plan—and it is an art, not a science—involves the founder in a delicate balancing process. On the one hand, a forecast is a representation of a fact—the founder's state of mind—and an intellectually honest founder will represent his state of mind accurately. Indeed, careless, let alone dishonest, preparations may involve liability. On the other hand, the forecast is a critical element in the negotiation process. Thus, as one prominent source on business-plan preparation (the *Arthur Young Business Plan Guide*) has noted:

> The entrepreneur should be careful to avoid negotiating in the business plan. For example, the entrepreneur who indicates he or she will sell 20

percent of the company for $200,000 has just established the upper end of the negotiating range. Sophisticated reviewers will realize that at worst they can acquire 20 percent of the venture for $200,000, and that they might be able to negotiate a better price.

The problem is that the forecast is an "indication" of price and value since it drives valuation, even though the business plan says nothing about "20 percent for $200,000." The standard language of venture-capital valuation (outlined in chapter 3) will be decoded by potential investors, reading the forecast as an offer by the founder to value his company at a given number. Consequently, it would be ingenuous to prepare a forecast without at least knowing how it will be read by the investment community. To be sure, if the founder does nothing more than work backwards in the forecasting process, targeting the valuations he wishes to achieve and then filling in the forecast behind that number, he may have made less than a bona fide effort to be candid. Nonetheless, ignorance of how the audience will react to a forecast is not bliss in the venture universe.

The answer, then, is that the forecast should be prepared with two considerations in mind. It should represent the founder's best thinking as to likely future events. But, at the same time, the founder should not close his eyes to what the consequences of his forecast will be; accordingly, he should at least understand how venture capitalists approach the forecasts in the context of the valuation process.

Thus, most venture capitalists contemplate a five-year time horizon, on the theory that an exit strategy is feasible at the end of five years. Therefore, the founder's forecast should go out as far as the investors are looking. Depending upon the maturity of the company and the ability of its product to excite, an informed founder can usually estimate what kind of compounded rates of return the venture capitalists are looking at over a five-year period. If, to reverse the example used in chapter 3, the founder "guesstimates" that the venture capitalist will be looking for a 38-percent compounded rate of return, a quick calculation shows the venture capitalist will be anticipating his investment will quintuple in five years. If the founder is planning to raise $250,000 from the venture capitalists, then the founder knows a forecast which shows anything less than $1 million in net after-tax earnings in Year 5 will mean he has to surrender more than 12.5 percent of the company. To illustrate, the venture capitalist can then be counted on to multiply one million times a price/earnings multiple (and that may be somewhere around 10, because, among other reasons, that number historically has often been seen in the marketplace and is easy to work with); once the venture capitalist comes up with a $10 million valuation, he will then calculate that his

$250,000 should be worth $1.25 million in Year 5 and find himself agreeing to take 12.5 percent of the company for $250,000 in Year 1 if and only if he sees (and believes) forecast earnings of $1 million or more in Year 5.

A final word on this point. Borrowing from the speech of Kenneth Olson to the 1987 M.I.T. graduating class, the forecast is both a prediction and a target. If you don't shoot high, the Law of Self-Fulfilling Prophecies dictates that you won't reach high. Exuberance in preparing one's forecast, if intellectually honest, is an integral part of a founder's mental terrain.

THE PROMISSORY NATURE OF THE FORECAST: "SHOOT LOW"

Lest one get the impression that the previous section baldly suggests the forecast should come out exactly where the founder wants it to, it should be remembered that professional venture-capital investors are not stupid. They will test the forecast and explore thoroughly the assumptions used, smoking out numbers that are intellectually dishonest, or, to put it in the vernacular, do not pass the "red face" test. A very steep climb in earnings in some remote period, for example, will be suspect. It being easier to kibitz a forecast in the early years, a spike upward in Year 5—when anybody's guess is as good as anybody else's—will reveal itself as result oriented. Moreover, an intellectually dishonest set of projections may provoke a negative reaction or outright rejection without further investigation. And, many investors view the forecast as a quasi promise by the founder, a representation that he proposes (albeit not legally bound) to make the forecast come true. The forecast is not so much a prediction of the future—five years is too long a time frame for precise predictions—but an undertaking by the party in control to accomplish a given objective. Indeed, a confident forecast of summary results may become a critical issue in the financing negotiations. Experienced investors are accustomed to confronting the founder with his rosy forecast, agreeing to a valuation based thereupon, and then insisting that a system of penalties be institutionalized, taking equity away from the founder if and to the extent he fails to achieve the projections he authored. As elsewhere noted, most venture financings entail multiple rounds, and, accordingly, are of the benchmark variety even if not explicitly so provided in the Purchase Agreement. The second-round investors, generally the same parties who invested in the first round, will be influenced in their pricing decision (in turn driving the founder's dilution) by the founder's record measured by the forecast. On occasion, the inability to meet an overly optimistic forecast may be the trigger for a control "flip," ousting the founder from office.

Section 2.10
Composite Table of Contents of Business Plan

1. Introduction (or Executive Summary)

   Short description of:

   Business objectives
   Principal products or services
   Technology and development program
   Market and customers
   Management team
   Financing requirements

2. Company description

   History and status
   Background and industry
   Company's objectives
   Company's strategies
   What makes the company different from others

3. Products

   Product description and comparisons
   Innovative features (patent coverage)
   Applications
   Technology
   Product development and R&D effort
   Product introduction schedule and major milestones
   Future products (product evolution)

4. Market

   Market summary and industry overview
   Market analysis and forecasts
   Industry trends
   Initial product(s)

5. Competition

6. Marketing program

   Objectives
   Marketing strategy
   Sales and distribution channels
   Customers
   Staffing

7. Manufacturing

8. Service and field engineering

9. Facilities

10. Management and ownership
    Founders and key employees
    Stock ownership
    Organization and personnel
    Future key employees and staffing
    Incentives (stock option and stock purchase plans)

11. Capital required and use of proceeds

12. Financial data and financial forecasts
    Assumptions used
    3-year plan
    5-year plan

13. Appendices
    Detailed management profiles
    References
    Product descriptions, sketches, photos
    Recent literature on product, market, etc.

One of the sections not specifically set out above which may be appropriate in the context of a given plan, is a "milestone" section, the forecasted major events in the life cycle of the enterprise and a timetable for their achievement.

chapter eight

You've Set up the Company and Negotiated the Price: What Are the Investors' Terms?

It is customary to begin the negotiation of a venture investment with the circulation of a document known as a "term sheet," a summary of the terms the proposer (the issuer, the investor, or an intermediary) is prepared to accept. The term sheet is analogous to a letter of intent, a nonbinding outline of the principal points which the Stock Purchase Agreement and related agreements will cover in detail. The advantage of the abbreviated term sheet format is, first, that it expedites the process. Experienced counsel immediately know generally what is meant when the term sheet specifies "one demand registration at the issuer's expense, unlimited piggybacks at the issuer's expense, weighted average antidilution"; it saves time not to have to spell out the long-form edition of those references. Second, since the term sheet does not purport to be an agreement of any sort, it is less likely that a court will find unexpected promissory content; a "letter of intent" can be a dangerous document unless it specifies very clearly, as it should, which portions are meant to be binding and which merely guide the discussion and drafting. Some portions of a term sheet can have binding effect, of course, if and to the extent an interlocutory memorialization is needed of some binding promises, that is, confidentiality of the disclosures made in the negotiation. The summary format of a term sheet, however, makes it less likely that any party will be misled into thinking that some form of enforceable agreement has been memorialized when it has not.

WHAT WILL THE VCS WANT FOR A SECURITY: COMMON STOCK? PREFERRED STOCK? DEBT? WARRANTS?

As one programs any financing, the objective, as in corporate finance generally, is to make $2 + 2 = 5$, that is, to obtain added value for the issuer. In the course of a financing, the insiders are, or course, attempting to raise the maximum amount of money for the minimum amount of equity, equity meaning claims on the residual values of the firm after its creditors have been satisfied. A corporation will issue at least one class of common stock because it must; many firms stop there; they pursue the simplest capital structure possible in accordance with the KISS principle ("Keep it Simple, Stupid"). However, in so doing, the corporation may close down its chances to pursue the added-value equation—$2 + 2 = 5$—because that equation involves matching a custom-tailored security to the taste of a given investor. The top line of the term sheet will ordinarily specify the security the VCs opt to own; the following discussion takes up the most common possibilities.

Different investors have differing appetites for various combinations of risk and reward. If a given investor has a special liking for upside potential leavened with some downside protection, the investor may "pay up" for a convertible debt instrument. An investor indifferent to current returns prefers common stock. Some preferences are driven by the tax law; corporate investors must pay tax at full rates on interest but almost no tax on dividends. On the other hand, the issuer of the security can deduct interest payments for tax purposes—interest is paid in pre-tax dollars—but not dividends. The sum of varying preferences, according to the plan, should be such that the issuer will get more for less—more money for less equity—by playing to the varying tastes of the investing population, and, in the process, putting together specially crafted instruments, custom made as it were. A potential investor interested in "locking in" a return will want a fixed rate on debt securities instead of a variable rate; the ultimate "lock-in" occurs in a zero coupon bond, which pays, albeit not until maturity, not only interest at a fixed rate but interest on interest at a fixed rate.

As the practice of tailoring—hybridizing, if you like—securities has become more familiar and frequent, the traditional categories can become homogenized. Preferred stock may come to look very much like common stock and debt resembles equity. In fact, the draftsmen of the Revised Model Business Corporation Act no longer distinguish between common and preferred stock. Moreover, it may be advantageous (again with a view to making $2 + 2 = 5$) to work with units or bundles of securities, meaning that an investor will be offered a group of securities, one share of preferred, one debenture, one share of common, and a warrant, all in one package.

Indeed, creativity by sponsors has spawned a variety of novel "securities," equity, and debt, which have played a role in venture capital, the underlying notion being to maximize values by crafting instruments to fit the tastes of each buyer and to capture current fashions in the market. The use of "junk" or "fluffy" debt has been the focus of popular attention of late; however, junk bonds—debt securities which are less than investment grade and, therefore, unrated— are only one species of the complex phyla of hybrid securities invented by imaginative planners. Thus, a given issuer's financial structure can perhaps be best envisioned by thinking in terms of layers of securities. The top layer is the most senior: usually secured debt, "true" debt in the sense that the holder is opting for security of investment and "buying" that security by accepting a conservative rate of return, a fixed interest rate, or a variable rate tied to an objective index. The bottom layer is the most junior: common stock (and if the common stock is divided into different series, the most junior series); on occasion, this level is referred to as the "high-speed equity." The risk of a total wipeout is the greatest, but, because of the effects of leverage, so is the reward. In between are hybrids, layers of securities with differing positions, meaning differing claims on Newco's current cash flows and the proceeds of a sale or liquidation of the entire enterprise. The variables open to the planners include the following: a security can be denominated either debt or equity with different tax consequences to both the issuer and the holders; a security may be senior, or subordinated, or both, as in senior to one level and subordinate to another (the term "subordinated" opens, in and of itself, a variety of possibilities); a security may be convertible into another at a fixed or variable rate of exchange (and convertible over again, as in debt convertible into preferred stock, in turn convertible into common); an equity security may contemplate some form of fixed recoupment of principal, perhaps expressed in terms of a redemption right, and redemption can be at the option of the issuer, the holder, or both; and the issuer's obligations to make periodic payments with respect to a debt security can range from the simple to the exotic—monthly interest payments at a fixed rate to so-called PIK payments (payment in kind, meaning in stock versus cash) tied to the performance of a particular business segment (as in so-called "alphabet" stock).

It is not feasible to cover the universe, since new additions and subtractions occur every day. The following discussion highlights instruments more commonly encountered, starting with the top of the pole.

COMMON STOCK

Common stock is the simplest form of equity security. It is not convertible, as a rule, into another type of security; each share enjoys one vote; dividends are payable without limit but only when declared by the board of directors; the common stock holder takes the last turn at the assets, or what is left of them, in liquidation. In a typical corporation, conversion privileges, as if obeying the Second Law of Thermodynamics, run downhill to the common; convertible securities are convertible into common either directly or indirectly, as when Series A preferred is convertible into Series C preferred, which is in turn convertible into common.

As suggested, a security called "common" stock can be complex, as complex as the draftsman wants to provide; there are no hard and fast rules except that there must be some class of stock with the residual voting, liquidation, and dividend participation rights. Two complex versions of common stock are frequently encountered: Class A common, which is, in fact, a form of disguised preferred without the special voting rights which some statutes require be inherent in shares labeled "preferred"; and junior common stock, a no-longer-favored security used for a time to get cheap stock into the hands of key employees at minimal tax cost. Class A common, being in fact a form of preferred stock, will be discussed below.

WARRANTS

A warrant is, like an option and a conversion privilege, a derivative security, a right to buy a security at a fixed (or formula) price: the "exercise" or "strike" price. A warrant is, in effect, a short-term option and, although often issued in connection with another security—debt with warrants attached—it ordinarily can be, by its terms, traded as an independent security. In contrast, an option, in venture-capital usage at least, is usually long term (up to 10 years) and personal to the holder because the typical recipient is an employee. A conversion right is a right to purchase stock which is inherent in another security—that is, a preferred stock or a debenture—and its characteristics are fixed in part by the security on which it is a parasite. All three labels refer to something which is, itself, a security.

Generally, neither the issuance of warrants nor their exercise (at least by nonemployees) is a taxable event. The IRS's earlier position that the expiration of a warrant occasioned a tax on the issuer was reversed by Congress in 1984. However, whenever a debt security with warrants attached is issued as a package, original issue discount problems are invited.

For a time, a popular financing device used by emerging companies starved for cash and business contemplated the issuance of contingent warrants, which become exercisable if and when the holder does something for the issuer—buys a given level of product, for example. That device is no longer as attractive, since the SEC has ruled in favor of current and periodic recognition of expense to the issuer.

For accounting purposes, a warrant, like an option, is considered a "common-stock equivalent," and, if it has been "in the money" (i.e., exercise price below market price) for three consecutive months, is deemed to impact earnings per share under the so-called treasury-stock method—that is, the warrants are deemed exercised, new stock is issued at the exercise price, and the proceeds to the issuer are used to buy in stock at the market price.

PREFERRED STOCK

Preferred stock comes in various shapes and sizes, depending on the intent and desires of the planners. Assuming it is so authorized in the charter, the board of directors may fix the rights, preferences, and privileges of the preferred, a practice creating what is known as "blank-check preferred." There are virtually no limits on the board's authority to frame a mosaic of rights and call the same a "preferred" stock. Some of the reasons to prefer (pardon the pun) preferred stock as a financing device have been discussed elsewhere in the text—that is, the "eat-'em-up" preferred, which makes possible price differentials between prices paid for stock by the investors and the founders. An overriding reason is convenience: although it is possible to work with other devices, it is particularly handy to use preferred stock as a mechanism to adjust the relationship between the cash and noncash investors; that is, to create specific rights in the cash investors such as special voting rights, antidilution protections, control shifts, "supermajority" veto provisions, and the like. A preferred stock can either be voting, nonvoting, or voting only upon certain issues, or upon the happening of certain events. In the case of the convertible preferred customarily issued in a venture financing, it is the norm to provide that the preferred votes pari passu with the common as if it has been converted. Beyond the preferred dividend, preferred stock in the instant context is usually "nonparticipating," meaning that earnings over and above the dividend are available to the common shareholders; the preferred holders' access to those earnings is postponed until conversion.

The traditional notion of preferred stock encompasses a share that takes its "par" value in liquidation before the common gets anything (a meaningful privilege if the company is being sold) and has a preferred call on the earnings of the corporation during its life in the form of a regular dividend. A "preferred" dividend implies a *fixed* dividend payable at regular intervals; if the dividend is not declared for any reason (perhaps illegality, if and to the extent sufficient earnings or surplus are not available), it "cumulates," meaning arrearages must be paid in the future before any dividend or liquidating distribution can be paid on inferior classes of stock, such as common. (Unlike interest, cumulative dividends are usually not augmented by an incremental additional payment keyed to the period during which they remain unpaid—interest on interest.) If cumulative dividends are passed for several periods, it is often (but not necessarily) provided that a "default" occurs and something automatically happens, usually in the form of the preferred shareholders getting additional seats on the board. "Participating" preferred (see below) is preferred that may or may not enjoy a fixed dividend, but in any event participates in excess earnings pari passu (or on some other formula) with the common shareholders.

Cumulative dividends expressed in cash terms are not common in start-ups. The idea of paying cash dividends at all makes no sense to some entrepreneurs (e.g., Kenneth Olson while at Digital Equipment), because the transaction is ultimately dilutive if and as the issuer, in effect, retrieves the capital paid out in dividends by issuing more stock. More importantly, immature companies often do not have the cash with which to pay dividends. Noncumulative dividends, meaning dividends paid only if, as, and when declared by the board, are the venture-capital norm. Indeed, the disclosure document in a preferred-stock venture financing often contains a caveat to the effect that the dividends are not only noncumulative, it is "unlikely" the directors will declare them at all. A start-up may, however, distribute future calls on earnings by providing for regular or irregular dividends on the preferred payable in stock, either preferred or common. This is one method of adjusting equity percentages based on performance of the company; if the founders have been missing targets, the board may be able to compensate the investors by voting the preferred some additional stock. These are, of course, traps for the unwary. Thus, preferred stock received as a dividend—the classic "preferred-stock bailout" or earnings—may become "Section 306 stock" which when sold turns capital gain into ordinary income. Moreover, §§305(b) and (c) of the Internal Revenue Code can create taxable events when a corporation distributes stock to its stockholders in a disproportionate way. Moreover, it is not clear that holders of preferred stock enjoy the same fiduciary protection as common shareholders.

The preferred's liquidation preference is not normally the occasion for much discussion in a start-up or buyout financing because none of the interested parties believe that distributions in liquidation of a venture-backed start-up or LBO will extend beyond the secured and unsecured creditors. On occasion, however, venture-backed companies may liquidate with proceeds available beyond the creditors' claims. Indeed, in insolvency proceedings involving substantial assets, something is usually thrown to the stockholders even though the creditors get less than 100¢ on the dollar. (The plan gives lip service to the "rule of absolute priority" in bankruptcy by giving the creditors cash plus securities "valued" at 100¢, leaving something left over with which to bribe the shareholders not to fight.) In such instances, the preferred liquidation preference may be significant. The preference also becomes significant if the issuer is merged into another company. The founder may argue that the preferred should be required to convert or be automatically converted prior to the merger—the merger is an "exit" vehicle. The investors, on the other hand, will argue that a sale of the company yielding an attractive price to the common stockholders will cause them voluntarily to convert; they are entitled to protection, on the other hand, if the proceeds are so meager that they do not cover the liquidation preference.

Automatic conversion on the eve of an IPO is usually less controversial. Indeed, it is often necessary to clean up the balance sheet and cancel various special rights peculiar to separate classes of stock if an IPO is to occur at all; those counsel who have survived a multiparty negotiation in which the holders (perhaps including former employees who simply detest the company) must be cajoled into converting can testify to the value of automatic conversion.

CONVERSION AND REDEMPTION

A nonconvertible preferred stock was, until recently, rarely encountered in the venture universe, where the idea of an unlimited "upside" drives the hopes and designs of the participants. Accordingly, preferred is often convertible into common stock (and, when it is not, the preferred is bundled with common stock, as discussed below, as participating preferred).

Conversion means giving up one security—the preferred, in the example—and receiving in return another, the so-called conversion stock, which is, in the typical case, common. There can be intermediate steps in the process—Class C preferred convertible into Class A preferred, which is convertible in turn into common—if the draftsmen have some reason to collect various classes of preferred into a single class prior to conversion into common.

Conversion is in many ways equivalent to the sale of the existing security and the purchase of conversion stock; a preferred (or, more likely, a debenture) with warrants attached gets the holder to the same place as a convertible preferred: ultimate acquisition of the conversion shares at the price paid for the security initially purchased. The principal distinction between stock with warrants attached and convertible stock is that the conversion privilege is viewed as "inhering" in the security itself, a defensible conclusion in the sense that the privilege cannot independently trade. A warrant, on the other hand, can be (and usually is) detachable from the security it originally accompanied, if indeed it was attached to any security in the first place. A warrant can, accordingly, be bought and sold on its own. One of the consequences of this distinction has to do with holding periods. The holder of a share of convertible preferred or debt is, for purposes of Rule 144, viewed as holding the conversion shares while, and for as long as, he holds the convertible security. Thus, if a holder has owned the convertible security for one year or more, and is not an "affiliate," he can convert and sell immediately within the restrictions of the rule. The holder of debt with warrants attached must wait for one year after he redeems the debt and exercises the warrants to sell the underlying stock.

Since a conversion right is a "heads I win, tails you lose" option in favor of the security holder, one which he will rationally hold until the last possible minute, the issuer naturally likes to mandate conversion as soon as possible. One way to force conversion is to include a right of redemption in favor of the issuer. If the convertible stock is more valuable than the exercise price—or "strike" price as it is called—then rational holders will convert in the face of a call. That option is not, however, the most realistic; start-ups lacking the cash may have no credible way to carry through on the threat to redeem. Accordingly, as earlier indicated, the preferred way to get rid of the preferred is to provide that it is converted automatically upon the occurrence of certain events (or the lapse of time). Automatic conversion, however, deprives the preferred stockholder of his choice.

For accounting purposes, convertible securities—whether stock or debt—are viewed as "common-stock equivalents" and, therefore, deemed converted for both the calculation of "primary" earnings per share and "fully diluted" earnings per share unless the yield—dividends or interest—is more than two-thirds the bank prime rate. Convertible preferred in the venture context rarely satisfies this test and thus impacts earnings per share under both tests, unless the effect of a deemed conversion would be antidilutive.

PREFERRED STOCK REDEEMABLE AT THE OPTION OF THE HOLDER

Investors in a start-up or buyout, no matter how well off on paper, ultimately need an exit vehicle. And with access to the initial public offering market only a contingent possibility in many phases of the market cycle, equity investors have been searching for alternative exit vehicles—that is, alternative methods for turning illiquid securities into readily tradable securities or cash. The fear of investors is that they will become locked into a company which shows no sign of either going public or going bankrupt—so-called walking-dead or lifestyle companies. Management will be content to run the company at a modest pace, neither making nor losing a lot of money, because it supports, in the jargon of the trade, their comfortable lifestyle. One of the countermeasures adopted by well-advised investors is to add to the typical convertible preferred provisions a right in the investors to redeem—that is, to put shares to the issuer after a period of time at a price which can be counted on to energize management into exploring all available alternatives. The typical convertible preferred does not pay current dividends. The redemption provision, however, will suggest a redemption price ordinarily at par (the amount paid for the preferred) plus some form of return on invested capital calculated as if dividends had been accrued and declared but not paid.

In structuring redeemable preferred, several concerns must be taken into account. First, the SEC has specifically addressed that type of security in Rule 5-02 under Regulation S-X. The SEC has in mind, among others, any security that is "redeemable at the option of the holder; or . . . has conditions for redemption which are not solely within the control of the issuer, such as stock which must be redeemed out of future earnings." The rule requires that redeemable preferred stock be separately identified in a note to the balance sheet and that such securities "are not to be included under a general heading 'stockholders' equity' or combined in a total with [nonredeemable preferred shares (meaning nonredeemable at the option of the holder) and common stock]." The Staff Accounting Bulletin repeats the Regulation S-X requirement that redeemable preferred not be included in shareholders' equity and goes on to suggest that the redeemable preferred should be assigned an initial "carrying amount" (i.e., the number at which the item is carried on the balance sheet) at fair value at the date of issue. If that fair value is less than the "mandatory redemption amount," then the "carrying amount" should be "increased by periodic accretions using the 'interest method' so that the carrying amount will equal the mandatory redemption amount." The "carrying amount" should also be increased by amounts representing dividends not currently declared or paid but which will be payable under the mandatory redemption feature, or for which ultimate payment is not solely in the control of the issuer (e.g., dividends that will be payable out of future earnings). The issuer is required to "highlight the future cash obligation attendant with redeemable preferred stocks through relevant footnote disclosure."

In comparing redeemable preferred stock with debt, certain other considerations need to be taken into account. Thus, even if the preferred redeemable at the option of the holder is not includable in "shareholders equity," the obligation to redeem will be reflected only in the notes to the balance sheet, not as debt on the face of the balance sheet itself. Moreover, since redeemable shares are not included in the "shareholders' equity" account, they are not considered outstanding for purposes of calculating earnings per share. Further, the holder of a preferred stock—indeed any stock—cannot petition the issuer into involuntary bankruptcy. On the other hand, in characterizing an investment as "stock," the issuer may encounter problems when it goes to redeem the shares under the pertinent state corporation law prohibiting stock redemptions absent adequate surplus. (Such restrictions do not apply to debt redemption since payment of debt is a balance-sheet wash; technically, capital and surplus are not disturbed.) The redemption of redeemable preferred appears, however, to be exempt from such prohibitions in some state statutes on the ground that creditors have advance notice of the possibility.

PARTICIPATING PREFERRED

The description of the typical preferred stock instrument obtained by the venture capitalists is not complete without describing a relatively new wrinkle in venture finance, the appearance of so-called participating preferred stock. If convertible preferred is the instrument of choice, the holder is left with the choice, upon an exit event such as the sale of the entire company, of holding on to the preferred instrument and being paid liquidation preference plus accrued dividends or converting and capturing the upside. Thus, for example, if a venture-capital fund has invested $5 million for 50 percent of a given company in the form of a convertible preferred security (convertible into 50 percent of the common) and the company is sold for $5.5 million, the holder of the preferred will, presumably, hang on to it and be paid the bulk of the proceeds to the exclusion of the common stockholders (e.g., the founder). If a company is sold, however, for any number significantly north of $10 million, then it is worthwhile for the convertible preferred to convert into common and share in 50 percent of the proceeds. Participating preferred, on the other hand, is of the "have your cake and eat it too" variety. Thus, the participating preferred is a straight preferred stock, with a dividend which, although not often paid currently, accumulates and is added to the liquidation preference as with a convertible preferred; however, the upside for the holder of the participating preferred stock is provided by a coincident tranche of common stock, meaning that, for the same $5 million, the investor obtains a straight preferred with a liquidation preference of $5 million *plus* 50 percent of the common stock, the securities aggregated into a "bundle" or "unit" as it is sometimes called. Then, if the company is sold for, say, $12 million, the participating preferred holder, instead of converting and obtaining $6 million in proceeds, with $6 million going to the common, gets its $5 million back plus accrued dividends of, say, $500,000 and then shares in 50 percent of the remaining $6.5 million. Accordingly, the common shareholders, instead of obtaining $6 million in proceeds, realize only $3,250,000. If the liquidity event is an IPO, again the participating preferred shareholder gets its money back plus accrued dividends and then holds 50 percent of the common stock, subject to dilution in the IPO.

If the liquidity event is in the hundreds of millions of dollars, the fact that the participating preferred holder gets the first $5 million back does not materially impact the common shareholders' internal rate of return. However, at numbers in the teens, the difference in return to the preferred versus the common is significant.

ANTIDILUTION PROTECTION FOR INVESTORS

In the "modern era" of venture capital—1970 and beyond—the so-called antidilution provisions have become increasingly important. Like so many words in the glossary of venture capital, "dilution" has multiple meanings. The core concept, however, arises from a central fact: any new claimant to the assets and/or income of a firm reduces the percentage interests of the existing claimants. Thus, if X and Y own 50 percent of a firm and Z purchases newly issued securities with a claim—say, of 25 percent—on future income, X and Y have been diluted in the sense that each necessarily owns a lesser percentage, a lesser claim. It may be, of course, that Z contributes cash or property in an amount sufficient to enable the firm to increase its earnings by, say, 40 percent. In such an event, it is arguable that X and Y's shares have not been diluted in the sense of watered down, because the firm enjoys surplus earning power. Nonetheless, their percentage interest, albeit in a larger pie, is smaller, and some would hold to the theory that X and Y have suffered in some sense.

Several Meanings of "Dilution"

The issue of dilution depends on what criteria are deemed significant in calculating value. If net earnings per share is the measure that drives stock price, then a financing which increases that result is nondilutive; if, similarly, cash flow or gross revenue per share is the critical indicator, the issue is, "Did that indicator go up or down on a per-share basis?" Some firms are given an overall bill of health in terms of return on equity or on assets; a dilutive financing is one that decreases that ratio.

The same analysis can be conducted in terms of book value. If the "shareholders equity" account is $1 million and X and Y each own 50 percent, the appearance of Z, who contributes $100,000 for a 25-percent interest, dilutes X and Y. If Z contributed $400,000 for 25 percent the financing is not normally considered dilutive; dilution in a balance-sheet sense is usually thought to occur only when net book value per share diminishes as a result of the financing. If Z lends the firm $1 million, it is arguable that the claim of X and Y is set back in liquidation, behind an additional layer of debt. However, since the firm has added the loan proceeds to the asset side of the ledger, dilution is not usually perceived as resulting in such instance.

The issue of dilution, however defined, arises in at least two contexts in venture finance. First, securities regulators, state and federal, are concerned that dilution be disclosed. The rules in this regard have in mind a balance-sheet test: net book value per share. The placement memo or prospectus should disclose what happens to the newly issued stock following the financing. If the price paid by the investors is $10 per share and net book value immediately after the closing is $5 per share (because shares were earlier issued to the promoters at $1), then dilution has occurred at the rate of 50 percent.

Antidilution Formulas

The very nature of a derivative security—a warrant, an option, a convertible preferred—requires some form of antidilution protection. Then, if a preferred share is convertible into ten shares of common and something happens to make the common cheaper, the preferred holder desires naturally to be entitled to *status quo ante*.

And, the easy part of the antidilution discussion has to do with recapitalizations (changes in the number of shares outstanding in the absence of an exogenous transaction such as a third-party financing or a consolidation with another firm; that is, stock dividends, stock splits, and reverse stock splits). These changes are technical. A 100-percent stock dividend doubles the number of shares and cuts the book value of the stock in half; absent a market reaction which reflects nonfundamental factors, one $20 share of stock becomes two $10 shares of stock. The more difficult issue arises when a later round of financing is at a lower price than an earlier round or rounds. Thus, assume the company sells preferred stock to investors in an early round, convertible at $1 a share, and then something changes. The issuer needs more money, as start-ups usually do, and so it sells more stock, perhaps common this time, at 75¢ per share. The preferred stockholders are diluted in a sense, but one may argue that such a contingency is a business risk. There were no guarantees when they bought their preferred. The "something" may have had nothing to do with the fortunes of the company; perhaps it is developing in accordance with the plan, but the investment climate changes. If the existing investors want protection against dilution, they can bargain for, and subsequently exercise, preemptive rights, essentially dollar averaging or averaging down to protect their percentage interest. After all, they are the people with cash to spend.

The foregoing is a plausible argument, but it neglects the Golden Rule (to repeat, "He who has the gold makes the rules"). Antidilution provisions tied to the price of subsequent financings operate at the expense of one particular class—the founder and his allies, the key employees—and to the benefit of the other class, the existing cash investors. The new investors, of course, do not care; they get the percentage of equity they bargained for at the specified price. They are either indifferent on the issue, or, because they overlap with the earlier cash investors, are in favor of antidilution protection. The founder has only one way to get rich, the horse he is riding, while the professional venture capitalists have a number of irons in the fire. The founder is, therefore, usually outgunned and gives up on antidilution provisions. Unfortunately, this can be a big mistake, a point to be revisited after an explanation of the way in which the provisions operate.

Full Ratchet and Weighted Average

There are two principal ways to formulate antidilution provisions, capitalizing the terms to make it clear we are talking about the ones which have substantive bite: the "Full Ratchet" and the "Weighted Average." Full-Ratchet provisions are the real killers, at least from the founder's point of view. They provide that, if one share of stock is issued at a lower price, or one right to purchase stock is issued at a lower aggregate price (exercise price plus what is paid, if anything, for the right), then the conversion price of the existing preferred shares is automatically decreased, that is, it "ratchets down," to the lower price. Depending on how many shares (or rights) are included in the subsequent issue, this can be strong medicine. A brief example will illustrate. Assume Newco, Inc. has one million common shares and one million convertible preferred shares outstanding; the founder owns all the common, and the investors own all the preferred, convertible into common at $1 per share. Newco then issues 50,000 shares of common at 50¢ per share because it desperately needs $25,000 in cash. To make the example as severe as possible, let us say the investors control the board and they make the decision to price the new round of financing at 50¢. Suddenly the preferred's conversion price is 50¢, the founder goes from 50 percent of the equity to just under 33.3 percent, and all the company has gained in the bargain is $25,000. Indeed, a Full Ratchet would drop the founder from 50 percent of the equity to 33.3 percent if the company issued *only one* share at 50¢. This is a harsh result, indeed. When a really dilutive financing occurs, say 50,000 shares have to be sold at 10¢ per share, the founder drops essentially out of sight. The company takes in $5,000 and the founder goes down under 9 percent, never to recover because he does not have the cash to protect himself in subsequent rounds. In the jargon of venture capital, he has been "burned out" of the opportunity. There is no other provision so capable of changing the initial bargain between the parties with the dramatic effect of Full-Ratchet dilution. When venture capitalists are referred to as "vulture capitalists," it is likely the wounded founders are talking about dilutive financings and a Full-Ratchet provision.

The more moderate position on this issue has to do with Weighted-Average antidilution provisions. There are various ways of expressing the formula, but it comes down to the same central idea: the investors' conversion price is reduced to a lower number but one which takes into account how many shares (or rights) are issued in the dilutive financing. If only a share or two is issued, then the conversion price does not move much; if many shares are issued—that is, there is in fact real dilution—then the price moves accordingly.

The object is to diminish the old conversion price to a number between itself and the price per share in the dilutive financing, taking into account how many new shares are issued. Thus, the starting point is the total number of common shares outstanding prior to the dilutive financing. The procedure to achieve the objective is to multiply the old conversion price per share by some fraction, less than one, to arrive at a new conversion price; the latter being smaller than the former, the investors will get more shares on conversion and dilute the common shareholders (the founder) accordingly. The fraction is actually a combination of two relationships used to "weight" the computation equitably. The first relationship is driven by the number of shares outstanding, the weighting factor, meaning that the calculation should take into account not only the drop in price but the number of shares involved—the significance of the dilution, in other words. (Call the number of shares outstanding before the transaction A.)

The fraction, then, takes into account the drop in price and expresses that drop in terms that can be mathematically manipulated with the first number to get a combined, weighted result. The relationship is between the shares which would have been issued for the total consideration paid if the old (i.e., higher) conversion price had been the price paid versus the shares actually issued (i.e., the shares issued at the new price). (Call these two numbers C and D.)

The combination of these two relationships—number of shares outstanding and the comparative effect of the step down in price (expressed in number of shares)—is a formula:

$$(A + C) \div (A + D) \times \text{Old Conversion Price}$$

If the shares which would have been issued at the old (i.e., higher) price is (as indicated) the number in the numerator, the fraction or percentage will be less than one. This fraction (say $1/2$ or 0.50) is multiplied by the existing (or initial) conversion price to obtain a lower conversion price, which means in turn that more shares will be issued because the conversion price produces the correct number of shares by being divided into a fixed number, usually the liquidation preference of the preferred stock.

It is open for theorists to argue about the fairness of that result, but the above formula has the advantage of economy of expression.

If one wants to use a Weighted-Average antidilution formula, the above is one commonly used (albeit sometimes expressed in different terms).

WHO CONTROLS: ME OR THEM?

To understand that cohort of issues which has to do with the control of a start-up, some background is in order. Thus, in a mature business corporation, it has been understood, at least since Berle and Means's seminal work, that nonmanagement purchasers of stock in public companies are passive investors. If they don't like the way the company is being run, their remedy (absent some actionable legal wrong) is to sell their shares. Venture capital operates on an entirely different set of principles. When raising money from his own investors—the limited partners in his venture pool—the professional manager of a venture-capital partnership holds himself out as someone with the expertise to "add value" to the investments under his control. The notion is that the typical founder is an incomplete businessman, with gaps in experience in matters such as financial management and marketing. An active board of directors, staffed by representatives of the investors, is expected to help fill these gaps. Significantly, even in successful venture-backed companies, a large percentage of the founders are fired, retired, or otherwise relieved of their duties prior to the company's achieving its maturity. It is rare to find the likes of a Ken Olson at Digital Equipment or an Ed DeCastro at Data General, executives with the necessary breadth and scope to take the company through every phase of its path toward maturity. Consequently, a term sheet will deal with a series of related control issues immediately after the question of valuation is tentatively settled.

A business corporation is, as a legal matter, run by its board of directors. In point of fact, many boards elect to yield the operational management of the company's affairs to a single individual, the chief executive officer, but the residual legal responsibility is not delegable. The board remains responsible. The president is a member of the board (under the laws of some states he has to be), and certain powers are delegated to him formally, usually in the bylaws. But the president's authority is derivative; to restate this important point, a seat on the board carries with it legal power and responsibility, whether the occupant likes it or not. In negotiating the term sheet, the struggle for power concerns who sits on the board.

That question breaks down into subissues. If the investors hold a majority of the stock but elect to retain fewer than 51 percent of the seats, when is it appropriate for the investors, assuming that they agree together as a group, to take over control? Regardless of who holds a majority of the outstanding shares, should the founder and his management colleagues retain control of the board until something objectively goes wrong, such as a failure to meet revenue benchmarks for X quarters, for example? The term sheet often unbundles the macroquestion of control and allocates the parts separately, across a spectrum of issues and across a period of time. Thus, it may provide that the investors may retain control over certain core questions—management compensation, for example—and not others. Further, the term sheet may provide for a control "flip," meaning that the investors are content with a minority of the board as long as everything is going well; they succeed to outright control of the board when and as the company gets in trouble, allowing them to tie a can to the founder. Control flip can occur when benchmarks are not met or for more serious reasons, such as the violation of negative covenants in a Stock Purchase Agreement.

From the investors' standpoint, control is a two-edged sword, since control entails some quantum of legal responsibility. Venture-capital investment is risky enough if all that has been put at risk are the dollars invested in the enterprise. If, in addition, an investor can be held liable to the creditors, and, indeed, to other investors, in an insolvent enterprise, his risk parameters are undoubtedly exceeded. Further, whether or not the liability is imposed by reason of the exercise of controlling influence, any board member has an assortment of "fiduciary duties," a phrase that, once appearing in a judicial opinion, usually takes on a precise legal meaning, that is, recovery by the plaintiff.

Apart from a few isolated decisions or special-fact situations generally involving lenders, it has as yet not been popular to impose liability, beyond the investment made, on investors who are deemed to be in control of a failed corporation unless they do something to impact directly on the minority, such as squeezing them out of the enterprise or feathering their own nests. Indeed, if such were to eventuate through the agency of activist judges making new law in line with their underdog sympathies, it would be a formidable problem for the venture-capital industry generally. The bulk of the cases to date have involved variations on the theme of the doctrine of equitable subordination whereby senior investors, those holding a debt security of some sort, have seen their priority vanish in an insolvency proceeding. The notion is that if the creditors take control of an insolvent company and manage its affairs so as to favor themselves, it is somehow inequitable to allow them to retain their status as creditors. Because of the heavy debt structure of leveraged buyouts, the doctrine of equitable subordination is much discussed in that arena. In start-ups, where the investors are not as prone to invest in debt securities, the doctrine is less intimidating. However, "fiduciary" liability in the event of a finding of control is an issue that cannot be ignored, particularly in view of the fact that directors and officers' liability policies are almost never affordable at the start-up stage (if, indeed, affordable at all).

Various provisions can be reflected in the term sheet to deal with the problem. Thus, some careful investors prefer to bargain for visitation or attendance rights for their representative on the board of directors, meaning the right to attend board meetings but not to vote. Occasionally, these rights are memorialized by calling the investor representative an "honorary" or "advisory" director. These measures should be viewed in context. The real power the investor group has over a cash-poor corporation is economic, not legal; the investors are the only source of fresh funds to keep the doors open. No law requires an investor group to advance fresh money (absent an agreement or except at the conclusion of a lawsuit holding it liable in damages for some form of misconduct), so the power of the purse rests with the investors. As it is sometimes phrased, the Golden Rule obtains: "He who has the gold makes the rules."

REGISTRATION RIGHTS

To comprehend adequately various issues involved, a discussion of basic principles is in order. The first is that registration rights are seldom used in accordance with their terms, and yet they are viewed by some investors and their counsel as a central element of the deal. The actual use of the demand rights, for example, could prove very awkward: a group of minority shareholders insisting on registration, the CEO agreeing only because he has to, but saying, in effect, to the minority, "Find your own underwriter, conduct your own road shows, do not bother me with questions from large institutional purchasers; in a word, sell the stock yourself." Such would make for a disorderly marketing effort, to put it mildly, and the price per share would suffer.

On the other hand, registration rights are often the only exit vehicle which, as a practical matter, the minority shareholders can compel. A start-up may issue shares redeemable at the option of the holder, but the instances in which that privilege has been successfully exercised are few. A company still in the development stage may not have the legal power, let alone the cash and/or the agreement of its creditors, to redeem stock. If a controlling founder is content to sit in his office, play with his high-tech toys, and does not need more money from his investors, the investors need leverage. There is no legal way, other than through the threat of enforcing the registration-rights agreement, to compel the company to go public. In this connection, it is important to keep in mind that liquifying the investors' shares through a public offering can be not only a promise, but also a benchmark; meaning that the remedy, if the founder refuses to cooperate, need not be a lawsuit. Reallocation of stock interests can be triggered if an IPO fails to materialize on time.

The second interesting feature of the registration-rights agreement is that it is, in point of fact, a three-way agreement, but with only two of the three parties negotiating and signing it. With a minor exception for "self-underwritten offerings," a primary or secondary offering of securities requires an issuer, selling shareholders, *and* an underwriter, either on a "firm" or "best-efforts" basis. However, the underwriter is usually not in sight when the registration-rights agreement is signed, and the parties themselves have to anticipate what the underwriter will require. Following that point, underwriters as a rule do not favor secondary offerings for early-stage companies. Given a choice, the market likes to see the proceeds of the sale go into the company's treasury, to be used for productive purposes, rather than released to outsiders. Moreover, whenever stock is being sold, the underwriter wants the number of shares issued to be slightly less than its calculation of the market's appetite. An underwriting is deemed successful if the stock price moves up a bit in the after-market. If the price goes down, the buyers brought in by the underwriter are unhappy; if it moves up smartly, the company is upset because the underwriter underpriced the deal. Consequently, the underwriter does not want to see new shares coming into the market shortly after the underwritten offering is sold, creating more supply than demand. These imperatives account for terms in the registration-rights agreement known as the "haircut" and the "hold back," meaning that the underwriter has authority to reduce the number of shares sellers other than the company are selling and to require that insiders eligible to sell restricted shares immediately under Rule 144, discussed in chapter 12, agree to refrain from selling for, usually, one hundred and eighty days.

Finally, including one's shares in a publicly underwritten offering is not the only way shares can be sold. A holder of restricted securities can sell his shares, albeit at a discount attributable to illiquidity, in a private transaction; more importantly, he can "dribble" out the shares into the market once the company has become public, under Rule 144. Registration rights for the holder of restricted shares in an already public company are, therefore, a redundancy unless the holder wants to sell before the required holding period in Rule 144 has expired or the block is so large that it cannot be "dribbled" out under the "volume" or "manner of sale" restrictions set out in that rule.

chapter nine

I Have a Letter of Intent: What's in the Contract?

The term sheet, in time, segues into a formal agreement. The understandings between the parties (as set out in the term sheet or simply by oral agreement) may be primitive: "Here's some cash, give me some stock." Nonetheless, any deal involving the sale of securities is legally complex because the law views that category of transaction in a special way; lawmakers and regulators, based on historical evidence going as far back as the South Sea Bubble, entertain deep concerns that there exist unusual opportunities for fraud and overreaching when the commodity traded is a security. Accordingly, the simplest investment contract—"one share, one dollar"—is in reality far from simple, since the agreement of the parties is complemented by rules imposed by statute and administrative regulation.

In a structured venture financing, the contract between issuer and investor is, or should be, detailed, covering a number of issues which otherwise may be the subject of future disputes and misunderstandings. The instrument recording the issues on which the parties' minds meet can bear any number of titles; it usually is called the "Stock Purchase Agreement" or "Purchase Agreement." The following discussion, consistent with the theme of the text, is designed to illuminate not only the various deal points but also the principles underlying the negotiations . . . where each party is coming from, in today's parlance, and what hangs on winning or losing a given point.

If artfully drafted, the Purchase Agreement, like any contract, tells a coherent story. Most legalese is rightfully condemned as "Bastard English," incomprehensible to the layperson. While there are, surely, some valid reasons for using what philosophers refer to as a "metalanguage" in legal agreements—"terms of art" in legal jargon—much of the mystery in legal drafting is unnecessary, the product of sloppy, lazy writers, or worshippers of archaic, out-of-date conventions.

For example, a contract, like a story, should start with an introduction, a paragraph or two which will set the stage and explain what the draftsman is trying to accomplish. Custom has it that the introduction should be segmented into a series of clauses, each introduced by the word "whereas," all of which makes the story jerky and difficult to follow. If the draftsman keeps in mind he is storytelling, he can readily perceive that the easiest and most understandable way to begin a preamble is with the label "preamble," followed by a consecutive narrative of the background of the transaction and a summary description. (The preamble is not, strictly speaking, a part of the agreement but the language is significant nonetheless, since, in case of a dispute, construction of the contested contract language will be influenced by statements in the preamble, to the extent material.) Calling a spade a spade, or in this case, a preamble a preamble, is not the only aid available to comprehension. A book has a table of contents for handy reference—the Purchase Agreement should as well.

The Purchase Agreement proper should open, again for purposes of clarity, with the basics: Who is buying what and at what price and when? The "who" are the investors and they are ordinarily designated in an attached appendix, a drafting device to allow changes up to the closing at a cost of retyping a single page. Even though subscribing en masse to a single document, the investors are, technically, each entering into a separate contract to buy stock. Usually, they are not responsible for any other investor welshing on the deal; their responsibility is, in legalese, "several" and not "joint."

The "what" is the security or bundle of securities being offered. If other than common stock—that is, preferred stock, warrants, convertible debt—often the most economical way to describe what is being offered is to attach the instrument itself and incorporate it by reference in an appendix, or a collection of appendixes labeled a "disclosure schedule." The danger in that practice, handy as it may be, is that a reader may overlook significant substantive terms by assuming that the appendix is "boilerplate"; that is, "a preferred stock is a preferred stock is a preferred stock." The fact is that many of the important points to be negotiated ("deal points" as they are called) are located in the document constituting the security, for example, the interest rate on the debentures and the conversion price. The moral of the story is to read and bargain out the appendixes; do not sign off on the Stock Purchase Agreement until the appendixes have been attached and carefully considered. Moreover, as discussed below, last-minute attachment of appendixes, as the parties are hurrying to close, is liable to provoke ill will as the issuer protests that counsel for the investors is nitpicking when counsel (often legitimately) points out that the appendixes introduce new substantive terms.

In this connection, if "units" are being sold—that is, a bundle of separate securities, debentures plus warrants, for example—it is only prudent to negotiate explicitly an agreed division of the purchase price and reflect that agreement in the Stock Purchase Agreement. This is usually a pro-investor provision; the investors want to mitigate "original issue discount." The idea of a mutually agreed allocation of the purchase price across the disparate commodities being sold is a subset of the general principle that parties to an agreement should specifically agree to take mutually consistent positions on matters of allocation (mutually agreeable filing positions on their tax returns, for example).

Describing the price is seldom a problem unless one of the investors is contributing property that requires valuation. The issuer sometimes insists the price be paid in "good funds" or "same-day funds," funds that are credited to its account the day of the closing so that "float"—that is, the loss of daily interest on the funds as they are being collected—is not the issuer's problem.

The "when"—the closing date—is usually straightforward: the date the cash is to be paid, the securities delivered, and the attendant paperwork completed. Some Purchase Agreements allow for multiple closings; indeed, this can be a significant element of the issuer's strategy on occasion. Thus, the problem, from the issuer's standpoint, in many start-up financings is delay; the investors will coo enthusiastic words in the founder's ear, exciting him to ecstasy, then sit on their hands while he edges closer and closer to the abyss. Occasionally, the tactic is deliberate; the terms may improve for the investors as the founder gets increasingly desperate. To counter investor lethargy, it is often advisable to admit the first investors as soon as they are willing to put up their money. Even if the proceeds have to be held in escrow, the fact of a closing often disciplines investors on the fence, the "train is leaving the station" effect.

If the transaction is being pushed at an accelerated pace, the Purchase Agreement may be signed and delivered and the closing take place simultaneously. More often, the closing is delayed while the securities are being sold, investors subscribing seriatim, or the investors sign as a group but conditions to closing (federal agency approval of a license transfer, for example) must be satisfied. It is sometimes necessary, after the agreement has been executed, to change the closing date, in which event it is handy if the subscribing investors have agreed in advance to be bound, as to this and other ministerial changes, by a single signatory—their special counselor—at any rate, by less than all of their number.

Multiple closings can also occur if the deal is of the "milestone" or "benchmark" variety, meaning that the investors parcel out the committed sums if and only if the founder is able to pass stated tests by specific dates. If the dates are missed, the founder is penalized by: (1) failing to be able to call down the later installment, (2) coughing up additional equity, or (3) a combination of the two. "Milestone" deals are characteristic of high-tech seed investments, when the viability of the entire project depends on certain technical hurdles being overcome. One milestone might be development of a prototype, the second a successful lab test, the third a successful beta test, such as proving out and debugging the device at a customer's location.

Some founders are nervous about milestone deals since they think the deck will be stacked against them in defining the milestones. However, viewed analytically, many venture financings are in fact, if not in name, of the "milestone" variety. Most start-ups are financed by multiple rounds: seed, first round, mezzanine, and so forth. The later rounds are, albeit not explicitly, based on milestones. If the existing investors do not think the company has made the necessary progress, they do not put up their money or do so at a reduced valuation. And, it is an article of faith in the business that no new investor will finance if the existing investors do not have enough faith to come forward as well. Therefore, in a very real sense, an explicit milestone deal favors the founder—at least he knows that if he does what he says he is going to do, he will get some more money at a specified price. In a conventional financing, the founder has only a reasonable expectation that more cash will come in if he "minds his P's and Q's." To be sure, nothing in the foregoing discussion should lead a founder to relax in negotiating a milestone financing. It is in the nature of the beast that ambiguities can creep into even the most rigorously defined scientific test.

A final note on closings. As indicated in the succeeding sections, the structure of the "representation and warranties" section is such that the majority of the language is in the agreement proper, but the substance is in documents which are attached, sometimes seriatim, to the main instrument—appendices or exhibits containing the problems which the issuer identifies as exceptions from the generic representations and warranties. Often the issuer will surface the all-important appendices on the eve of the closing, accompanied by urgings that the investors' counsel not "nitpick." To avoid this unwanted pressure, the investors are well advised to insist the closing date be the later of the scheduled date or some period, say forty-eight hours, after the appendices are exposed.

Traditionally, after the deal has been described, the Purchase Agreement plunges into the issuer's representations and warranties, one of the longest sections in the Agreement. This is the section with which lawyers inexperienced in venture financings feel most comfortable, and the overwriting in this section becomes almost competitive. Thus, investors' counsel from one of the major New York firms, accustomed to billion-dollar merger and acquisition transactions, will write in representations dealing with multiemployer collective-bargaining agreements for a company with two employees. The way to approach the representations and warranties section, accordingly, is to understand the underlying dynamics.

By way of introduction, representations and warranties are not designed to serve the same purpose in venture finance as in giant merger and acquisition (commonly abbreviated as M&A) transactions between solvent investors and issuers. If the start-up issuer misstates its balance sheet to prospective investors, the inclination of the damaged investors to seek restitution must be restrained because the guilty party, almost by definition, will be out of money. As an aid in making aggrieved investors whole from the pockets of the issuer, the representations and warranties in an early-round financing are usually a bust. Moreover, it is arguable that explicit representations and warranties are superfluous, since the investor enjoys common-law remedies for the tort of deceit and statutory protection under Rule 10b-5 of the '34 Act. Why, then, bother with elaborate representations and warranties?

First of all, the section is designed, although not explicitly, as a device to draw into a lawsuit, given a misrepresentation, the perennial "deep pockets" in the financing: the law firm, the accountants, and the investment bankers (if any) serving as placement agents. Although the representations as to the financial statements are made by the issuer and the issuer alone, the existence of the representation makes it plain, if the question were ever in doubt, that the investors were relying on the accuracy of the statements, and that all the ancillary parties engaged in preparing the Purchase Agreement are, or should be, aware of such reliance. Since reliance to one's detriment has historically been an element of a plaintiff's case in the tort of deceit (although not universally required in the modern cases), memorialization in writing of the investors' reliance may obviate problems of proof. The issue of *scienter*—a claim by the issuer that it did not know of the critical omission—is also avoided by explicit "warranties." Further, those representations that have to do with the legal facts surrounding the issuer's existence—its due organization, the number of shares outstanding—form the reference point for an opinion of issuer's counsel validating those propositions which counsel are in a position to verify; again, a deep pocket if a damaging error is made. (A point of particular interest in a high-tech start-up will often be counsel's opinion concerning the validity of the patents, copyrights, or trade secrets protecting the issuer's technology.) Moreover, participation in the process of preparing the written representations—drafting the language in the case of counsel—may be enough to draw counsel into the zone of responsibility as a matter of law; the lawyers become "participants" in the entire transaction. Similarly, the founder can sometimes be induced to endorse certain of the representations personally, putting his pocketbook (for what that's worth) behind the statements made. If the founder balks, claiming he cannot be held to know certain facts absolutely, a representation can be softened to a so-called knowledge rep—that is, "to the best of my information and belief"—thereby catching the founder who is demonstrably lying. If the founder cannot pay in cash, the worst case is that investors can pick up some or all of his equity.

The representations also serve to motivate all hands—founder, investment bankers, lawyers, and accountants—to reexamine the facts. This is an incontestably salubrious use of the section: to energize these parties to do their investigations carefully so as to minimize subsequent disputes. In fact, if the investors want to make (as they usually should) their own investigations—an "acquisition audit" as it is sometimes called—they may be deterred by a fear that the issuer will attempt to defend a charge of misrepresentation by claiming the investor is estopped by its own inquiries. Unconditional written representations, perhaps accompanied by a statement that the investors may rely on the same even in light of their own audit, serve to diminish that concern.

The representations serve an important ancillary function: as closing conditions. Assuming that the Stock Purchase Agreement is not closed simultaneously with its execution, the investors will be able to withhold their investment if they discover imperfections in the period between execution and closing. In fact, one of the traditional representations is to the effect that there will be no materially adverse change in the issuer's business between signing and closing, which gives the investors an "out" even though the issuer has told the truth throughout.

Finally, the warranty flavor of the representations and warranty section indicates the function of these provisions as a risk-allocation device. Thus, it assumes a contingency the warranting party *did not* know about and *could not* have known about. The resultant loss is the responsibility of the warranting party even though the representation was not, at least consciously, untrue.

Sometimes the agreement becomes confused between the company's *representations* and its *covenants*. Conceptually, the two are quite different. The company "represents" facts—that is, existing statuses. When it "covenants" something, the obligation is promissory; the company is promising to do (or not do) an act in the future. In both cases, the company is liable for breach, but the damages are technically different. A misrepresentation entails tort damages while failure to perform a covenant opens up contract damages. It is not unusual to find promissory statements mistakenly included in the representations and warranties section; viz., "The company's insurance policies are as listed on Exhibit A" (a representation), and/or "the company will maintain those policies in force" (an affirmative covenant). This is a problem principally for the draftsmen of the complaint when and if the agreement is involved in litigation.

The covenants divide into two categories (affirmative and negative) and onto two levels (ministerial and very serious). The ministerial covenants, usually affirmative, have to do with promises the company can keep with relative ease: sending out reports and the like. Breach of the same usually involves only corrective action. (Occasionally, a covenant concerning a control issue will find its way into the Stock Purchase Agreement; that is, "the company will elect X, Y, and Z, nominees of the investors, to the board of directors." This is usually a rookie mistake. The agreement between the company and the investors is not the place for that type of promise because the company does not elect people to the board, the stockholders do; such provisions belong in the Stockholders Agreement.)

Certain negative covenants are also within the clear power of the company to observe, and are, in that sense, ministerial. Thus, typically the company promises it will not engage in certain major activities absent investor consent—for example, payment of dividends, fees to insiders, large borrowings, new issues of stock, mergers, changing management salaries, firing a given officer, redeeming shares; such negative covenants buttress and enlarge the statutory requirements that certain significant proposals—that is, mergers—be put to a shareholder vote. The issues can be important and worthy of spirited debate, but the point is that the promisor—the company—can still exercise control over its destiny. It is unlikely the company will violate them if only because the objecting shareholders can restrain any breach.

The covenants that the company cannot control, the more ominous covenants, are those of the loan agreement type, for example, the company will maintain a given net worth and/or specific asset-to-liability coverage. These promises, which can be stated affirmatively or negatively, are dangerous because they are beyond anyone's control; moreover, they usually entail specific remedies. The investors need not start litigation since a well-drafted agreement provides them with practical compensation (in addition to and not in lieu of their other remedies); that is, control of the company "flips" in their favor and/or the founder gives up stock, the equity equivalents of acceleration clauses in a debt instrument.

A popular form of managing risk entails a form of contingent payment, depending on the postclosing performance of the entity. The principal issues involved are negotiation of the earn-out formula and protection of the investors against a cooking of the issuer's postclosing books, whether deliberate or inadvertent, which will cause the formula to work against the interest of the investors. An earn-out formula may simply refer to the earnings of the issuer "according to generally accepted accounting principles" after the closing; but the matter should not be, and usually is not, disposed of that simply. Draftsmen have to deal with what Gilson calls "nonhomogenous expectations," if, for example, there exists a substantial amount of goodwill on the balance sheet of the issuer, the question is whether the amortization of goodwill should impact the formula. Other items to be covered in such negotiations include the depreciation schedules to be employed; treatment of extraordinary charges; the appropriate method for valuing inventory; whether or not to capitalize or expense items such as research and development; and changes in historical practices such as the treatment of pension costs. The formula should also reduce, to the extent possible, the rewards of gaming—for example, management's attempt to manipulate the indexes during the earn-out period.

Securities law issues include the question whether the receipt of contingent stock involves a new investment decision and, therefore, the need for separate registration (or an exemption) and the appropriate holding period under Rule 144 for nonaffiliates vis-à-vis the contingent stock.

From the investors' point of view, one advantage of "earn-outs" is obvious: if the issuer has breached a surviving representation or warranty, the investor may set off against its earn-out obligation (or any deferred payment) versus chasing the issuer or its shareholders for the money.

STOCKHOLDERS AGREEMENT

It would be technically possible to include all the provisions of the term sheet in one agreement, the Purchase Agreement discussed above, but it is usually not convenient to do so because of the several parties to the financing documents—the company, the founder, the investors, and the key employees; usually none are parties to all the promises entailed in the financing. If counsel were to draft an umbrella agreement, it would be necessary in each subsection to specify not only who was promising what, but to whom and with whom, and to make sure that no party to the umbrella agreement inadvertently wound up becoming bound to a promise that he lacked the power to perform. Accordingly, the Stock Purchase Agreement is usually accompanied by a Stockholders Agreement, an agreement by and among the founder in his capacity as a stockholder and the investors. The company may, on occasion, be made a party to this Agreement for the sake of convenience, but usually only in a supportive role.

A principal reason for a separate Stockholders Agreement, as earlier suggested, is that the company does not control who sits on its managing board, the board of directors; an agreement signed by the company purporting to govern who sits on the board would be circular in the sense that the subordinate would be pretending to exercise power over the supervisor. Therefore, it is advisable to record the understandings, if any, on that important issue in an agreement to which the holders of the majority (or, better, all) of the voting shares of the company are parties, since the board is elected by the stockholders. In its simplest form, the stockholders will get together (all or a majority of them) and agree to: (1) maintain a board of X number of people; and, (2) either elect specified individuals to the board, or, more commonly (and prudently since individuals are mortal and/or they change their minds about serving on boards), specify how representation on the board is to be allocated among the stockholders. The common stockholders, for example, will be allocated X number of directors and the preferred stockholders, *Y* number; each class of stock will be given the power to remove their own directors and replace them as they see fit. The agreement may, further, provide for a so-called control flip, meaning that if the fortunes of the company deteriorate, the preferred stockholders will get more board seats, either vesting control in them for the first time or reinforcing their already-existing control.

RIGHTS OF FIRST REFUSAL

As earlier suggested, the corporate charter is often the appropriate place for first-refusal options in favor of the corporation. However, the corporation may not be interested in exercising those rights (or may not be able to do so) and, consequently, the investors often bargain for first-refusal rights in their favor in the Stockholders Agreement. Such provisions can become quite complicated if a group of investors and issuers are involved. Assume that the founder wants to sell a specified number of shares to a third party. The investors (assuming that there are several) may have differing appetites for purchasing the founder's shares at the price that has been tendered by the third party. Some may want to buy and some may want to drop. Under those circumstances, the Agreement will ordinarily provide that the investors initially have the right to take up their pro rata portion of the offered block, and then, when somebody passes, those investors with the remaining appetites have a second bite of the apple and, indeed, a third and fourth, until the wishes of all the investors are satisfied. The founder is then free to sell the remainder at the price specified during some reasonable period of time. In that connection, when a stockholder, including the founder or any one of the individual investors, dies, an estate-tax problem arises to the extent the shares are illiquid. Taxes must be paid and the shares cannot be sold except at a discount. One method in dealing with the problem is to create a "put" in the estate of the deceased individual shareholder to sell the stock to the corporation, or, failing the corporation's ability to purchase, to the remaining principal stockholders. If the company is the party responsible for putting up the cash, the "put" ordinarily would be reflected in the Stock Purchase Agreement. If for any reason, however, the founder has negotiated for his estate to "put" shares to some of the heavyweight investors, the Stockholders Agreement would be the venue for recording that portion of the deal between the parties.

chapter ten

Selling Stock, Privately . . . and Legally

The so-called §4(2), or private-offering, exemption is the basis on which most emerging business enterprises are able to sell securities in the United States. (The term refers to that section in the '33 Act which contains the exemption.) Because of a series of fundamental miscues when the legislation was first drafted, the '33 Act reads backwards. Instead of postulating a definition of exempt private offerings, or defining the offerings which must be registered, the Act suggests that all sales of securities are to be registered and then exempts various transactions, including ones "not including any public offering" of securities. Since by far the great bulk of transactions are of the exempt variety, the tail is wagging the dog. Were the language to be interpreted literally, a crime wave could break out in this country as unsuspecting small businessmen, raising a few dollars from friends and relatives for the classic corner fruit stand, wind up invoking the civil (and, theoretically at least), criminal sanctions for violations of §5 of the '33 Act.

For many years, the corporate bar urged the SEC to define the entire process by which securities move from the issuer to the investors so that private transactions could go forward with certainty. Until relatively recently, the Commission stoutly resisted. The SEC repeatedly denied, for example, the persistent notion that sales to twenty-five or fewer persons constituted a private offering and clung to the conceptually immaculate—but practically untidy—view that "offerees" were the key indicator, a slippery criterion since the federal definition of "offer" was and is much broader than the common-sense construction of that term would indicate. Faced with a variety of devices cleverly calculated to mask disguised offers, the SEC's announcements are replete with language suggesting that the merest hint could constitute "indirect solicitation."

During the period of uncertainty, practitioners worked out their own guidelines, with little help from the SEC, to determine when a placement was exempt. This body of learning continues to be marginally pertinent, since the new rules, while providing a "safe harbor" (a well-used term in the law) for certain issues, do not replace the less certain parameters of §4(2) for offerings that cannot fit under the black-letter rules of Regulation D, described hereafter.

Thus, in 1982, after almost forty years of tugging and hauling, the law finally came to a sensible resting place; the Commission-promulgated Regulation D, or "Reg. D" as it is called, which provides a practical "safe harbor" without a host of difficult traps for issuers and their counsel.

Reg. D is not exclusive. For placements unable to fit within the black-letter rules of Reg. D, §4(2) continues to be available. However, the thrill has largely gone out of this area of practice. We are dealing now with private offerings with thousands of offerees and hundreds of purchasers; some such private offerings result in instant public companies, required to register (because they have more than 500 shareholders) under §12(g) of the Securities Exchange Act of 1934. The SEC has at last come to the point one expected it would never occupy—administering a rule offering relative certainty, a rule which authorizes the issuance of billions of dollars of securities annually in major transactions without the benefit of public registration.

Reg. D, which covers solely primary, or issuer, transactions, breaks down into six sections. Rule 501 is a definitional rule; most important is the definition of "accredited investor," which is any person within one of following categories:

1. Institutional investors: banks, insurance companies, investment companies, broker/dealers, thrift institutions, business development com-

panies, SBICs, certain employee benefit plans, and certain 501(c)(3) charitable corporations.

2. Insiders: directors, executive officers, and general partners of the issuer.

3. "Rich" individuals: natural persons whose joint net worth at the time of purchase exceeds $1 million or whose individual net income was over $200,000 ($300,000 if joint) for each of the preceding two years, coupled with a reasonable expectation of that income level for the current year.

4. "Rich" entities: any corporation, business trust, or partnership with total assets in excess of $5 million if not organized for the purpose of making the investment, plus any private trust with assets in excess of $5 million, not organized for the purpose and directed by a sophisticated person.

5. Aggregates of the above: any entity whose equity owners are entirely accredited investors under any category.

Rule 501's other key provision relates to the calculation of the number of allowable purchasers in an exempt transaction. Accredited investors are excluded from the count, meaning that there may be, with limitations explored in this chapter, an unlimited number of accredited investors.

Rule 502 sets forth the general terms and conditions to be met if Reg. D is to apply. It specifically addresses integration of contemporaneous offerings, the information to be provided investors, and limitations on the "manner" of the offering and/or resale. Rule 503 adds the notice requirements on Form D, to be filed by the issuer with the SEC no later than fifteen days after the "first sale" of securities.

The exemptions themselves are contained in §504 (issues of $1 million or less), §505 (issues of $5 million or less), and §506 (all other issues).

The antifraud provisions still apply to all transactions, and therefore Reg. D does not do away with the necessity for disclosure (although disclosure requirements are relaxed in some instances). It is also important to note that the burden of qualifying for the exemption has not been shifted; it is still up to the issuer and its advisers to make certain that each of the requirements of Reg. D has been complied with. However, the SEC has caved in to the argument that substantial compliance should be enough to maintain the exemption's applicability. In sum, not only is Reg. D an enormous help to issuers and their counsel, but the SEC has also been forthcoming in explaining the rule. In a release published on March 3,

1983, the staff issued an extensive interpretation in question-and-answer format. A number of no-action letters have further fleshed out the bar's insights into the staff's views. Reg. D itself is, as rules go, quite specific; it's possible, indeed, for a layman to understand the major provisions of the rule simply by reading it. Since its original promulgation in 1982, there have been a number of relaxing improvements. Thus, in 1988 the definition of "accredited investor" was enlarged, and the Rule 504 exemption ostensibly increased from $500,000 to $1 million. In 1989, the SEC deemphasized the filing of Form D (no longer a condition to the exemption, although still required to be filed); adopted a change to the effect that, in Rule 505 and 506 offerings with both accredited and nonaccredited investors, the specified information need only be supplied to the nonaccredited investors (one wonders what lawyer would be brave enough to furnish material to some but not all investors in a placement); and finalized Rule 508, the "excuse me" or "innocent and immaterial" (I & I) rule, which allows issuers to be forgiven for committing violations of Reg. D which are "insignificant" and occur despite a "good-faith attempt" to comply. And, in 1992, as part of the Small Business Initiative, the limit on the Rule 504 exemption was effectively raised to $1 million, and securities issued in Rule 504 transactions are no longer "restricted" securities.

The rules (Reg. D is a "regulation" comprising a series of "rules") ostensibly allow for the issuance and sale of securities to an unlimited number of purchasers (culled from an unlimited list of offerees) if they qualify as accredited investors, meaning people who are rich or otherwise qualified in the eyes of the SEC. Contrary to all prior learning, Reg. D (with exceptions having to do with the way prospects are identified) is not *technically* offended if the placement is made available to an unlimited number of offerees, a dramatic departure from the SEC's former view. Given a pool of "rich" people and a presanitized prospect list, an issuer can make what amounts to a public offering—with perhaps as many as a thousand or more purchasers of the security and some multiple of that number as offerees—without technically running afoul of Reg. D.

A critical caution is in order at this point, however. Regardless of the number of purchasers (maybe even none) or offerees, if the placement is made on the basis of either "*general* solicitation" or "*general* advertising," then an unregistered public offering may have occurred. Obviously, it's hard to get a deal in front of even a limited number of potential purchasers without participating in some kind of activity reasonably viewed as "solicitation." The problem facing a founder approaching Reg. D is how to keep from running afoul of the ban on "general" solicitation and yet get his business plan out widely enough so that he has a chance of raising the money.

The first rule of thumb in this area is almost a banality, but it is one that bears constant repetition: keep careful records. An analysis of the cases in which issuers were held to have gone beyond the bounds of §4(2) will show varying fact patterns, as one might expect, but, in the author's view, one consistent theme pops up: the issuer and its agents did not keep careful records and, therefore, were unable to state with certainty when challenged in court how many people had been offered the opportunity. Continuing that tradition, in a 1985 SEC enforcement proceeding under Reg. D involving an illegal general solicitation, the order prominently reflected the fact that the number of persons solicited was not known because the issuer's records were so inadequate.

Secondly, it goes without saying that the ban on advertising, even though stated in terms of "general advertising," really means no advertising at all; since it is difficult to conjure up a practical scenario involving "nongeneral" advertising—it is an oxymoron. Thus, announcements of the offered opportunity in the newspapers, on the radio, on television, and so forth, are not in order. One would think that this constraint was clear enough—either you trumpet the investment opportunity in the media or you don't—but nothing in life is simple when the securities laws are involved. An ambiguity is likely to arise if, for example, the technology being exploited is interesting and the press wants to do an interview with a founder naturally proud to have come up with a scientific breakthrough. In theory, if the founder limits his conversation with reporters to the technology and makes no mention of the fact that he's out hustling to find funding, the media have not been used "in connection with" the sale of a security. The problem is that one hasn't control of what a reporter will actually publish; a single mention in the press of the pending offering could inadvertently blow Reg. D's safe harbor. In a 1985 no-action letter commenting on so-called tombstone advertising (an ad which does no more than give the barest of information), the staff restated its view that materials designed to "condition the market" for the securities constituted an offer even though the tombstone did not specifically mention the transaction in question. (The risk, I hasten to add, is not likely to be SEC enforcement, as the discussion below indicates; the danger is that a disgruntled investor will initiate a civil action based on an allegation that the "safe harbor" is unsafe.)

Even with the most careful records, a forbidden solicitation may still be alleged because the word "general" is not susceptible of a precise, objective test. For example, a founder may want to mail to a list of, say, all venture-capital funds named in *Pratt's Guide to Venture Capital Sources*, the most common reference book in the field. If a mailing does go out to a thousand names, is that a general solicitation? The SEC has helped illuminate the issue in a series of no-action letters. Taken together, the letters indicate a staff view that general solicitation does not occur when the solicitor and his targets have a nexus: as the SEC puts it, a "substantial preexisting" relationship.

The learning comes largely from the tax-shelter syndication area, where placement agents with long lists of previously screened prospects are the norm, because, at least prior to 1987, tax-shelter "junkies" (as they were called) tended to be repeat buyers. Thus, in a factual pattern which runs through the no-action responses most often cited as influential, it is typically brokers, not the founder, who are soliciting individuals to invest in limited-partnership products. In order to establish a meaningful "preexisting business relationship" between the broker and the prospect, the brokers send out "cold" mailings well in advance of the deals—questionnaires asking individuals to fill in certain financial information and to establish a record of their "sophistication" in such transactions. Reading the requests together, the staff's view is that an offering not in existence at the time the questionnaire was mailed can be sent out widely without running afoul of the general-solicitation constraint.

However, a founder doing his first, and perhaps the only deal of his lifetime has no access to a list of prior prospects. Absent such a list, the founder is left to soliciting his friends, business acquaintances, and parties with whom he can conjure up a prior relationship of some kind. Presumably, that list can be expanded vicariously, by asking his lawyer, accountant, and/or banker to make the material available to potential purchasers with whom they are acquainted. How much further he can go is still unclear. Parenthetically, as was earlier indicated, it is critical to keep careful records identifying all offerees, even though the names do not appear on a master mailing list. If an intermediary is asked to help, it is important to memorialize the intermediary's activities.

Finally, while the foregoing discussion exemplifies the law, at least according to the face of the statute, the rules, and the reported precedents, there has appeared in recent years a phenomenon, which this writer on occasion has jokingly labeled a "crime wave," which needs to be taken into account. That is to say, for years the classic view among practitioners was that there could be no mention in the public press or in public forums of a pending private offering. The term "gun jumping" is sometimes applied in this context, although it appears in other legal contexts as well. When confronted with an inadvertent leak to the press about a private offering, the more cautious law firms would insist that the placement come to halt, a cooling off period ensue, and the solicitation efforts be not restarted until the effect of the unauthorized and unfortunate public announcement had been vitiated by the passage of time. There has been no explicit change in the rules but, nonetheless, there has been an *implicit* movement away from that notion. That is to say, there appear routinely in the trade press (such as *The Private Equity Analyst* and local publications such as *Alley Cat*) issuer-generated reports of private placements in process, sometimes specifying the amount of the capital being solicited. Moreover, at the venture-capital clubs and other public forums in which companies seeking private equity present themselves, obviously the potential investors are attracted by public media announcements, mass mailings, ads in newspapers, bulletin-board presentations, and the like. The SEC appears to be looking the other way, except perhaps in the event of blatant fraud; therefore, since no law firm can appear to be "holier than the Pope," experienced counsel are themselves overlooking public announcements and presentations which otherwise would qualify as general solicitation and advertising and disqualify the placement.

IF REG. D IS NOT AVAILABLE?

While Reg. D has proven in practice to be extremely useful in aiding venture-backed placements, not every issue can or will be sold in compliance with the exemption. Reg. D specifically provides that it is not exclusive; thus, §4(2) is (at least theoretically) available in time of need. Certainly, however, the occasion for sole reliance on §4(2) will be infrequent. If Reg. D is lost because there has been a "general solicitation," one can hardly imagine the circumstances that could encourage the issuer to turn to §4(2).

Reliance on §4(2) standing alone is most likely, first, in those gilt-edged placements (the classic instance of a limited placement to a small number of highly sophisticated institutional investors) when compliance with Reg. D is deemed to be a bother. The issuer does not feel it necessary to qualify the investors as accredited or to file Form D. The second major category is after-the-fact justification, a common problem in venture finance. When Start-up, Inc. was organized, the founder was unaware of either Reg. D or §4(2) and thus complied with none of the formalities. Some years later, when Start-up, Inc. is ready for an initial public offering, it will be necessary for counsel to recreate the exemption, as it were, in aid of its opinion that the initial issue was not in violation of the securities laws. Ex post facto compliance with Reg. D is not usually an option, leaving §4(2) as the only available alternative.

The gist of §4(2) is that it focuses on offerees. For the exemption to obtain, each person to whom the investment opportunity is exposed, each offeree, must fit within one or more of the special categories. Those categories have been developed in the case law revolving around the central notion developed in the *Ralston Purina* opinion, that the disclosure requirement entailed in a registered offering should only be relaxed if all the potential buyers were of the type that they could "fend for themselves" in the sense that each could develop "access" to the information a statutory prospectus would provide.

For many years, the courts, counsel, and the SEC staff have danced around the fend-for-themselves conception without reaching a test that was, or is, entirely satisfactory. As former SEC Chairman Ray Garret has noted, the principal element in the equation—the "saving recipe" as he called it—has remained a moving target, a "brew" made up of a number of elements but lacking an agreed-upon, objective list of ingredients. There is, however, a consensus on the identity of the elements going into the brew, what facts the courts have deemed important in the past, albeit no consensus on the weight to be accorded each one.

Thus, it is clear that the offerees as a class should have one or more special abilities which give them the power and/or ability to obtain access to information about the issuer and to process that information intelligently. At one extreme, a director of the issuer, particularly one sophisticated in financial matters, is almost certainly an eligible offeree. On the other hand, the mere fact that the offerees are employees of the issuer is not (without more) sufficient to invoke the exemption; this is the holding of the *Ralston Purina* case.

Over the years, the idea of the "sophisticated" investor has crept into the folklore of §4(2), a concept now enshrined in the requirement that nonaccredited investors in Reg. D offerings of more than $1 million have "such knowledge and experience in financial and business matters as to be capable of evaluating . . . the merits and risks of the prospective investment." In the strictest sense of *Ralston Purina*, a "sophisticated" or "smart" investor might have no power to obtain access to information because the issuer either did not have it, or would not supply it. However, the "smart" investor presumably would know how to factor in the dearth of information in making an investment decision.

Moreover, the "smartness" of the offerees is one, and only one, factor in the "recipe." Thus, the number of offerees has always been deemed important, although not determinative, since an offering involving as few as one offer, at least conceptually, could be outside the scope of §4(2) if the other factors in the "brew" so militated. Counsel were led to follow the suggestion of the SEC's general counsel in an early opinion that twenty-five or fewer offerees constituted a safe harbor, but no authoritative court or Commission pronouncement ever adopted that number as a rule. As stated above, one factual thread runs through many (if not all) of the instances in which a nonfraudulent offering was deemed outside the scope of §4(2); that is, the defendant issuer was unable to show how many offers had been made because it had failed to keep records.

The number of offerees is ultimately related to an important, and obvious, factor: the manner of the offering. If an offering is made using the traditional media of public offerings—advertisements, open seminars, paid salespeople, extended mailings, cold calls—it stands to reason that a public offering is in progress. The desire of issuers, particularly in the tax-shelter area, to reach out to a wide number of potential purchasers has often stretched this criterion, prompting counsel to creative heights with such devices as "screening." Again, as stated above, screening involves the idea that there are allowable techniques for prequalifying potential investors (thereby reducing the number of offerees), which do not rise to the dignity of an offer and, therefore, can be conducted more or less with impunity. One notion is to send out a private placement memorandum from a deal already closed and inquire of the recipient whether he would be interested in an investment resembling the "dead" deal; another is to circulate an offering only to financial advisers—lawyers, accountants, investment advisers—to induce them to disgorge names, coupled with an admonition that the deals are not to be shown to the clients until authority is given by the issuer. Since these questions are now being addressed in a series of no-action letters construing the general solicitation ban in Reg. D, it is likely that all subsequent learning will be developed in that venue. Reg. D being viewed generally as an expansion of the ambit of §4(2), counsel recommending that an issuer who cannot use Reg. D because of the ban on "general solicitation" may nonetheless resort to screening under §4(2) will be taking an unusually aggressive position.

Finally, the §4(2) exemption, like Reg. D, is conditioned on the nonexistence of a subsequent public distribution. The investment-letter device, coupled with a legend on the stock certificates themselves, should be employed in private placements generally.

chapter eleven

Compensating Your Key Executives

THE "CARROT" APPROACH: EQUITY INCENTIVES

Since both start-ups and buyouts depend in large part on extraordinary performance by managers qua proprietors, one principal aim of the planners of new ventures is to put stock or stock equivalents in the hands of senior managers without occasioning tax liability. Indeed, managers may be required to accept stock instead of cash compensation in order to preserve cash flow for the benefit of the lenders. The trick is to use stock as currency without occasioning immediate tax, not a simple exercise since, in the final analysis, stock is being awarded for past or future services, a taxable event in classic terms. Second, the equity should be allocated, if possible, in a way that has minimal effect on reported earnings. In this connection, a majority of the commentaries on this issue are written by tax practitioners; when a compensation scheme enables the company to take a tax deduction, they view that as an unalloyed "plus."

All other things being equal, of course, tax deductions are favorable. But if the cost of casting a system in a given way is a "hit" to earnings as reported to shareholders, then it is time to revisit the question. Thus, an option should not be weighted exclusively by the after-tax effect on the recipient, the grantee. The fact is that the chief value of a stock option under today's rules may be the option's effect, or better, its lack of effect, on the grantor. Until the Financial Accounting Standards Board (FASB) changes its rules, the grant of stock options as a form of employee compensation impacts the income statement as of the date of the grant, which is to say not at all, since the value of the option itself as of that date is indeterminate if the grantee's exercise price is equal to "fair value." As the option grows in value, culminating on the day it is exercised, the grantor's earnings are unscathed (FASB lost the battle, which unfortunately turned political, to charge compensation expense earnings as options increase in value; the compromise relegates disclosure to the financial statement footnotes). By way of contrast, a phantom stock plan, which periodically awards to employees "units" ultimately redeemable in cash (the value of the units being tied to stock performance), can have an enormous negative impact on earnings. (To be sure, any issuance of rights to purchase shares has a potential effect on the all-important earnings-per-share number.)

The issue on this head can be of startling importance. Upon an exit event, meaning a sale of Newco or a Newco IPO, the price paid is usually calculated as a function of current and historic earnings. For every dollar in GAAP earnings lost, the exiting shareholders, including the employees concerned, may well sacrifice large upside dollars in accordance with the price/earnings ratio then applicable—$10, for example, if the P/E ratio is 10 to 1. Indeed, recent calculations show that the costs to some public companies, where executive options are repurchased (i.e., replaced) with cash, is in the billions of dollars.

A central planning imperative is to tie equity to the performance of the employee. Thus, if shares (or options or stock equivalents) are awarded, it is important that employee "fat cats" are not thereby created, employees who can relax from and after the date of the award and watch their colleagues make them rich. Accordingly, awards, once made, usually "vest" over time, meaning that the price is fixed as of the date of the grant, but the options or stock can be recaptured for nominal consideration if the employee elects to quit prematurely.

Regardless of how sophisticated the stock or stock-option plan may be, it is likely that the employee will have to pay tax at some time on the value he has received. The trick is to match the employee's obligation to pay tax with his receipt of income with which to pay the tax.

STOCK OPTIONS

A "stock option" is a right issued to an individual to buy shares of stock in a given issuer at a fixed or formula price (subject to adjustments) over a stated period of time. It is a "derivative" security in that the option itself derives its value from the value of the underlying stock. An option and a warrant are conceptually the same; an option is a warrant exercisable, usually, by an employee and usually over a longer period. An option is usually issued by the company itself, to be satisfied by newly issued stock, but such is not necessarily the case. Any owner of stock can sell an option—a "call," in trading parlance—on his stock on whatever terms are mutually agreeable, but the same will not be an "incentive stock option."

To the company planning on issuing the options, there are several events in the process (each of which could be the occasion for a tax of some kind). If the option is to enjoy favorable tax treatment (and perhaps even if it is not), the first step is for the directors to adopt, and the stockholders to ratify, a stock-option plan. Adoption of a plan does not, of and by itself, involve the grant of options to any individuals. The plan, first and most importantly, identifies the maximum number of shares which can be issued to all the recipients in the aggregate; this is usually about 10 percent to 15 percent of the total stock outstanding, depending on the caliber of the employees and the willingness of the investors to dilute. The plan tells the stockholders the maximum amount of dilution they will suffer if all options are granted and exercised. It also sets out the basic provisions in each option contract, most of which are required under the Code if the options are to be "incentive stock options" under §422.

Options are granted to individuals pursuant to individual contracts. The scope of the plan contemplates the issuance of incentive stock options (ISOs) and/or nonqualified stock options (NSOs) and, perhaps, cash buyouts of the options in lieu of exercise, in the discretion of the issuer or the employee (Stock Appreciation Rights, or SARs).

INCENTIVE STOCK OPTIONS

Incentive stock options (usually abbreviated as ISOs) are rights to purchase stock structured to comply with the requirements of §422 of the Code. If the requirements are satisfied, the holder, who must be an employee of the issuer, will not be subject to federal income tax either at the time of the grant of the option or at the time of its exercise; and gain realized on a sale of the underlying stock will be capital gain.

Incentive stock options must be issued pursuant to a "written plan" which includes the aggregate number of shares to be issued and the eligible employees (or class of employees). The option plan must be approved by the shareholders within twelve months before or after board approval, expire after ten years (five years in the case of a 10-percent stockholder), be granted pursuant to a plan less than ten years old, carry an exercise price equal to current "fair market value" (110 percent of such value if the optionee is a 10-percent stockholder), and be nontransferable. An incentive stock option may provide that the employee may exercise his option by paying with stock of the issuer and he may have a "right" to receive "property" in lieu of stock at option exercise. The exercise price in each contract will be fixed at "fair market value" of the stock at the time an option is granted. The grantee will have no more than ten years from the date of the grant in which to elect whether or not to exercise the option, which means, in effect, that the option will not ordinarily be exercised until the tenth year, since the prime virtue of an option is that it allows the investment decision-maker to postpone his decision until the last instant. Eligible grantees include only employees of the corporation and the options are not assignable. The rule that incentive stock options on no more than $100,000 worth of stock could be granted in any year was redefined by the Tax Reform Act of 1986 so that, effectively, the plan can grant options at the outset on $1 million worth of stock, but the amount of options which vest in any year during the ten-year period cannot exceed $100,000. The effect of this provision is to allow the same amount of options per individual as under the old rules, but to validate the use of the earliest possible (and presumably lowest possible) exercise price throughout. The oldest options need no longer be exercised first, a significant benefit in any scenario in which the price of the issuer's stock fluctuates both up and down and options are granted sequentially.

Usually, the plan also establishes a committee of the board (not including anyone eligible to participate in the plan) to "administer" the plan—that is, to grant the options—and sets up a system for tying options to performance. Dribbling out grants of options over a period of time can work to tie rewards to performance, but such a procedure means, in a rising-share-value scenario, that the grantee's exercise price will escalate. Hence, the better-drafted plans over-grant the number of options in the early stages (a procedure made easier by the Tax Reform Act of 1986, as earlier indicated) and then provide for "vesting"; that is, the power of the issuer to recapture granted options lapses in decreasing amounts as the employee's longevity increases. Once an employee terminates or is terminated, he must exercise his options (only those vested, of course) within a short period: usually a month (and not, by law, more than three months) after termination, meaning he loses the ability to postpone his investment decision. (On the other hand, to preserve ISO status, he must hold the option stock for one year before selling it.) The short fuse on post-termination exercise increases the possibility that a terminated employee's vested options will be allowed by him to lapse (and go back into the pool for someone else).

NONQUALIFIED STOCK OPTIONS

Nonqualified stock options (NSOs) are "nonqualified" in the sense that they do not meet the requirements of §422. Unlike incentive stock options, the holder will realize ordinary income upon exercise equal to the excess of the fair market value of the stock received (as of the date such stock is free of substantial risk of forfeiture or becomes transferable, according to §83 of the Code) over the value of the consideration paid. Without incurring cash expense, the employer will be entitled to a business-expense deduction equal to the amount of compensation taxable to the employee. The holder's compensation is not a tax-preference item for purposes of the alternative minimum tax. The employer will have a charge against its earnings if, as of the date of grant, the fair market value of the shares subject to the option exceeds the exercise price.

Since few specific legal requirements are applicable to the issuance of nonqualified stock options, great flexibility is permitted in the terms of such options. The following features are typically found in nonqualified options due to applicable state and federal tax and securities laws:

1. The price may be at or below market price at the time of the grant.

2. Only a minimal holding period is required, to meet general state-law requirements of adequate consideration.

3. The employee's ability to exercise the option need not be limited to the period of employment.

The option is (usually) not transferable except by will or the laws of descent and distribution—although such is not required except by some residual fear that a freely transferable option may entail taxation at the date of grant.

ISOs versus NSOs

The principal advantage of an ISO is that it postpones tax on the holder's gain (exercise price versus sales price) until the option stock is sold; the tax on an NSO holder occurs upon exercise, measured by the difference between exercise price and fair value as of that time. This is a major distinction. The NSO holder has to come up with his tax money earlier in the process, provoking a potentially unacceptable investment risk unless he can sell immediately after exercise. However, as per Rule 144, he cannot sell publicly; that is, he must either hold for one year or sell at a stiff discount, unless he is able to register his stock for sale. Indeed, the interaction of the Code and Rule 144 can produce a script Yossarian could appreciate. On exercise, the NSO holder owes tax on the difference between exercise price and fair market value—calculated without regard to the restriction which will lapse; that is, the inability to sell publicly for one year. Let us say the trading price of the stock is $10 and the exercise price is $6. Tax is owed on $4 of gain. Mr. Yossarian can sell right away in a private transaction, but at a gain of, say, only $2. He has to pay tax on $2 of gain he cannot then realize, forcing him to choose an immediate sale at an economic loss so as to develop a countervailing loss for tax purposes. Alternatively, he can pay his tax and hold the stock for one year and sell without a discount, but—Catch-22—the stock may have gone down in price in the interim. He has paid tax on a gain he has not seen and, one year later, he may have an economic loss in the stock because the price falls. Moreover, the deduction for interest on the money he has borrowed has been severely limited. He gets a tax loss after a year of agony, but, by that time, he may be broke. On the other hand, the holder of an NSO may have an advantage *if* the Rule 144 holding period is not an issue because his employer has made the necessary filing to allow an immediate sale of the underlying stock into the public markets (the required registration statement is on Form S-8). In that event, the holder can pursue "cashless exercise," meaning he can take the option to a broker who will advance the exercise price, sell the stock, and remit cash in the amount of the spread. The penalty is ordinary income tax rates, but the risk of holding the stock for any period is gone.

There is more, however, to the comparison between ISOs and NSOs. The second major advantage of the ISO over the NSO—that the gain on sale was capital gain if the stock is held for a year after exercise (and the sale succeeded the grant by two years)—was rendered relatively immaterial by the 1986 Tax Reform Act, since the differences in tax rates became relatively small to the point of triviality.

However, with the 1993 Deficit Reduction Act, the distinction has been significantly restored and ISOs are back in fashion. Moreover, if the option stock is "qualified small-business stock," it may be that the spread will be even more dramatic. On the other hand, exercise of an ISO produces tax preference in an amount equal to the difference between the "fair market value" of the stock on exercise and the amount paid unless the option stock is sold in the year of exercise—an event which voids preferential treatment under §422. This feature led some commentators to forecast the death of ISOs. The alternative minimum tax (AMT) result is not, however, an unmitigated disaster since, in most instances, the excess tax paid is recovered when and if the option stock is subsequently sold at a gain. Finally, under the 1993 Deficit Reduction Act, the spread on NSOs will enter into the calculation of executive compensation for purposes of measuring whether the $1-million threshold has been achieved and, thus, deductibility disallowed. The short of the matter is that, in an era in which the tax law changes annually, there is considerable luster to what might be called the "wait and see" approach. According to that strategy, the issuer constructs a plan involving ISOs. Then, as some critical date nears—an IPO looms, for example—the employee enjoys alternatives. He can exercise the option and hold the shares if alternative minimum tax is not a problem as a practical matter, thereby postponing tax while the Rule 144 period runs, or he can do something to disqualify the option as an ISO—sell before the one-year holding period lapses, for example, assuming an S-8 is on file.

In this connection, the situation must be addressed from the issuer's point of view as well. A corporation is not allowed a deduction at any time in connection with ISOs granted to its employees (unless there is a disqualifying disposition of the ISO). A company can deduct the amount of ordinary income an employee is deemed to have received in connection with an NSO at the same time ordinary income is includable in the employee's taxable income. The value of the deduction allowed to a profitable corporation in connection with an NSO may well exceed the value to the executive of an ISO over an NSO. Perhaps the issuer will want a tax deduction and would be willing to pay the employee a bonus, accordingly, to make a disqualifying disposition. Moreover, in the event of a disqualifying disposition, the gain is the lesser of the putative gain on exercise or the actual gain on sale. And, as indicated, the accounting treatment of NSOs and ISOs is the same; a "hit" to earnings only if the option is granted at less than fair value, at least until the FASB rules change.

The point is that there is no one right answer to the ISO/NSO decision, particularly in view of the uncertainty posed by the FASB proposals and the irresistible impulse of politicians to tinker with the Internal Revenue Code; it is impossible to set out any general rules. The ISO versus NSO question should be examined carefully in light of the facts of each case and the tax, securities, and accounting rules in effect at that time.

"GROSSING UP"

An employee may be issued stock at bargain prices (or for free), plus a cash bonus in an amount sufficient to allow the employee to pay tax on the bargain purchase element. This is a relatively simple transaction called "grossing up." The result is that the employee gets the stock, after all taxes are paid, at the bargain price he agreed to pay and the employer, since it is paying the employee in cash, has a pot from which to withhold and, accordingly, take the deduction. The problem is that "grossing up" costs the company money at a time when cash may be scarce and it debits earnings when every drop of reported income may be precious in valuing the company's stock.

MISCELLANEOUS ITEMS

There are any number of variations on the foregoing themes, including the issuance of junior common stock (no longer favored), so-called haircut programs, book-value stock plans, phantom stock plans, ESOPs, stock bonus plans, and the like, several of which raise tax, accounting, and ERISA issues well beyond the scope of the text.

THE CARROT-AND-STICK APPROACH: THE EMPLOYMENT AGREEMENT

In the early stages of a company's existence, opposing principles should be balanced in the planner's mind. First, since the unseasoned firm is so dependent on critical people, it is important to tie those employees—the key ones at least—to the company as tightly as possible. It must be kept in mind that the founder and some of the key employees carry the business around in their heads. If they are free to walk out, to set up a new and competing business on the other side of Sand Hill Road in Menlo Park or Route 128 in Lexington, the investors may find that their entire stake has been sacrificed. On the other hand, the savvy planner also realizes that many of those in the first wave will ultimately be fired or passed over. With rare exceptions, the skills required to go from birth to adolescence are not the same as those needed to carry the firm to and through adulthood. The scheme, from the company's point of view, must take into account the real possibility that the very employees who are so critical to early success will be redundant in the later phases. An employment contract is analogous to one of Donald Trump's prenuptial agreements: What does one pay in advance for a divorce?

The contract between the company and its key employees is a highly significant document in venture finance. It specifies salary and other benefits, of course, but the well-drafted version goes far beyond those topics. It deals with control of the company's future and protection of vital assets, including the people who possess the intellectual property which is the backbone of many a start-up firm.

An employment contract reads as if Mr. Smith is being promised a long-term position with Start-up, Inc., for an annual salary plus, perhaps, equity in the firm, in consideration of Smith's promise to perform as, say, CEO for five years. Neither promise, however, is exactly what it seems. Realistically, Start-up's board of directors is saying to Smith, "If we want to fire you, we will pay you X dollars for your equity and Y dollars to buy out the remainder of your contract." Smith is saying to Start-up, "If I decide to quit, you can get some of your stock back for nothing and the rest for Z dollars, plus a restraint to keep me out of your business for, say, one year."

The contract, in other words, is like a prenuptial agreement. As long as the parties are happily married, no one reads the document; the principal issues have to do with the payoff numbers when divorce ensues—what are the partners' remedies in the case of breach? Professor Harold Shepherd at Stanford Law School used to divide his course offerings on the law of contracts into two distinct sections: one having to do with the formulation of the agreement and its administration, and the second, which he labeled "Remedies," having to do with the rights of the parties in the event of breach. Employment agreements, because they are not specifically enforceable in the sense of requiring the parties to remain married, become interesting when they fall into Shepherd's latter category: What to do in the case of breach.

Termination and Expiration

In discussions of the employment relationship, confusion often crops up, creating troublesome misunderstandings when the agreement is reduced to writing. If the employee demands a "three-year" contract, that means either: (1) he is promised a salary from, say, January 1, 1994, through December 31, 1996, meaning that the employee is contractually guaranteed a salary over an ever-decreasing amount of time;

as of, say, October 1996, the salary protection has shrunk to a matter of months; or (2) alternatively, a "three-year" contract means that the employee is hired on January 1, 1994, and is entitled to what amounts to three years' severance pay *whenever* he is terminated other than for cause or by his voluntary act. The employer, in effect, has issued an "evergreen" promise to pay him three years' salary regardless of when termination occurs, the day after he is employed or ten years after. When considering the merits of each scenario, one has to go back to the point that the employment arrangement centers around the cost of buying out the employee's contract. With an evergreen provision, that cost is constant. Employment for a fixed term, on the other hand, makes it easier for the employee to be fired the longer he is with the company and thus fails to give the employee a fixed level of protection. Therefore, a multiyear employment contract usually refers to the evergreen arrangement; strictly speaking, the employee is terminable at will, subject to the severance arrangement. Assuming that the parties' minds have met on the term of the severance, the remaining issues concern price—what events give rise to the obligation of one or the other parties to pay a penalty, and in what amount?

Damages

This discussion started with a proposition that equitable relief is not generally available to compel a firm to continue to employ a given individual (versus paying his salary) for the agreed-upon period or to compel that individual to continue to report for duty at the firm. However, there are indirect ways of achieving that result, by working with the concept of damages. Thus, if an employment contract were to provide that, upon the early termination of a given employee, damages in the millions of dollars would be payable by the firm, that employee, in effect, would enjoy an insured lifetime position because he would be too expensive to fire. Alternatively, if an employee wishing to quit were faced with a provision in his contract that imposed on him an enormous penalty, then he (if able to respond in damages) would be indentured to the firm for the same reason. In fact, except in large public companies (where a multimillion award to a departing CEO may be immaterial to the annual financial results of the firm), huge penalty buyout provisions are uncommon. A start-up cannot afford to be locked into a seven-figure settlement amount for dismissing an individual. A typical provision contemplates that the employee will be paid the balance of his salary, either in a lump sum on a discounted basis or during the balance of the period remaining in the contract. From the company's perspective, while the employee's flight may in fact imperil enormous investments, it is questionable whether a court would enforce a huge liquidated damage provision against the employee.

One of the principal reasons for stating the measure of damages is that the parties can, as they should, agree explicitly on the sticky issue of the employee's duty of "mitigation." If the contract is silent, it is not clear whether a given court will (or will not) find that the terminated employee has an obligation to mitigate the employer's damages by finding other employment, setting off the employee's new salary against the employer's obligation to pay the old. A duty to mitigate damages, whether express or implicit, includes subsidiary issues: What kind of position is the employee obligated to take? How much effort must he devote to looking for a new job? Where can he be required to take a job? In another city? When the issue is squarely addressed in a contract (as it should be), the possibilities to be covered in the drafting are lengthy. In addition to the ones mentioned, what if the employee elects, after termination, to manage his investments? If mitigation is contemplated, should the income from those investments be counted as if it were a salary? What if he is able to resell his vested equity in his old firm at a profit and then finds himself investing the proceeds in a new start-up, serving as chairman of the board of directors? Do director's fees count as salary, particularly if the former employee is devoting most of his time to the new company? The terminated founders of start-up companies are often young men who have interesting business careers in front of them, albeit not of the conventional kind. It is tricky, therefore, to forecast all the kinds of income that should count against the obligation of their former company.

Equity Recapture

Often the most potent penalty imposed on a footloose employee is the recapture of nonvested equity, either options or cheap stock. If the draftsman employed by the company has kept the main chance in view, he will recall that the object of an employment agreement is multifaceted: to stimulate the employee's current performance and to keep out of his head visions of sugar plums dangled by competing firms. If valuable equity can be recaptured at a penalty price when the employee quits, the term "golden handcuff" becomes apt. It is awkward to provide that the employee who terminates before his promised time has to pay a cash penalty back to the company; he usually does not have the resources to spare and it is more trouble than it is worth to the company to chase him for some sort of cash "cough-up," even though the injury to the investors may be substantial. On the other hand, the vanishing employee may cause the investors to lose their entire investment, perhaps running into millions. The better weapon used to avoid that unhappy result, therefore, is to string out the vesting of equity incentives as long as possible and to provide for forfeiture in the case of the employee's breach. It goes without saying that the employee's power to assign shares subject to forfeiture must be openly and notoriously restricted; otherwise, the possibility of forfeiture could be neutralized by a transfer to a bona fide purchaser whose lack of knowledge cuts off the forfeiture restraint. Further, it is customary to distinguish the level of recapture, depending on the occasion. If, as the earlier discussion assumes, the employee quits voluntarily—in the worst case, to join a competing firm—or is fired for cause, then the most severe recapture is called for. If the employee is fired for reasons other than cause, or dies, then either no provision is made or a modified quantum of nonvested stock is affected.

RESTRICTIONS ON POST-EMPLOYMENT BEHAVIOR: NONCOMPETITION, NONDISCLOSURE, AND "WORK-FOR-HIRE" CLAUSES

The legal literature on occasion deals with certain promises between an employer and its employees—noncompetition, nondisclosure, and ownership of inventions—as if they were entirely separate arrangements, involving discrete legal principles and policy considerations. In fact, in the usual case, all three are closely interrelated, one might even say variations on a single theme. And, at the risk of some confusion for those accustomed to separate presentations, the discussion in the text will frequently treat them as if they were part of one whole.

The critical issues arise generally after the employment relationship is terminated. That is to say, if an individual is in fact a current employee, there is little controversy about an obligation, either expressly or by implication, not to compete and to maintain his employer's secrets in confidence. Once the employee is out on his own—either fired or by his voluntary act—how far can the employer impose restrictions on his subsequent behavior? Can the employer prevent him from joining or organizing a competitive firm and/or disclosing confidential information? Can a noncompete clause be considered a permissible surrogate for a nondisclosure obligation, on the theory that a ban on competition is the only effective way to police the confidentiality undertaking? Can the employer assert ownership rights to inventions the employee comes up with, even those invented (at least ostensibly) after the relationship has been severed? Does it make a difference whether the employer is relying on common-law principles of unfair competition, a state statute (perhaps a version of the Uniform Trade Secrets Act), or express contractual provisions?

Labels: "Noncompete" versus "Nondisclosure"

Depending on the state laws obtaining, it may be a bad idea to style any term of the employment arrangement baldly as a "covenant not to compete" (unless, as discussed below, the covenant is imposed in connection with the sale of a business or a significant stock position). Competition is the American way; labeling a restraint as anticompetitive is simply asking for some court to find a way around it in the clutch. Careful legal work, therefore, should start with the title of the section in the employment agreement, denoting what it is precisely the company is trying to accomplish: a "covenant not to misappropriate proprietary information," perhaps, in which case the noncompete restriction is structured as a buttress, a way to enforce a nondisclosure obligation which cannot otherwise be realistically patrolled.

Indeed, there are multiple reasons why courts and legislatures are hostile to noncompetition agreements. Strictly enforced, the provisions could mean that the former employee cannot make a living in his field. Moreover, many of the most glamorous start-ups were the brain children of free spirits, who left giant oaks to plant little acorns. If IBM had elected to impose, and been allowed to enforce, noncompetitive clauses in every possible instance, one wonders what the computer industry in this country would look like today. Prudent counsel should start, therefore, with the presumption that a covenant not to compete may be unenforceable (pending, of course, a thorough review of state law). Instead of drafting language without substantive impact, the search should be for provisions which will survive, which have a fighting chance of accomplishing some corporate purpose when a valued employee leaves.

The issue, of course, can be serious. The flight of the scientific brains of the company into the arms of a competitor can be a death sentence. If a choice has to be made, the investors are well advised to let the provisions of, say, the registration rights agreement pass without negotiation, directing their counsel to focus in on this area. Given the high level of judicial and legislative hostility, it is sensible to frame each contract individually, tailor-made to the particular employee and the threat he poses, once on the loose, to his former employer's prosperity. If he is to serve as the marketing manager, the agreement should zero in on avoiding the harm that an individual in that post can do; perhaps a prohibition on the former employee aiding another firm in contacting customers he cultivated while in the plaintiff's employment. A court is much more likely to enforce a restraint if it is carefully limited to the potential injury facing the employer; this requires that thought be given to each individual case. Off-the-shelf provisions are unlikely to accomplish their stated objective.

It should be noted that emotions run extremely high in these disputes. The work atmosphere in a high-tech firm is often intense; the key officers work so feverishly and such killing hours in the development of a new technology that their bond is as close as the marriage sacrament. When one of them decides he owes it to himself to strike out on his own, the emotions can be extremely bitter, the investors and officers of the earlier firm viewing the defection as hideously unfair if the defector is able to parlay his knowledge and experience into the building of a competitor, as is so often the case. Tying employees to a firm for life may be good and accepted practice in Japan, but it conflicts with the mobility built into U.S. society. On the other hand, for investors and employees of a given firm to see their hard-earned secrets walk out the door and form the basis for a clone across the street is unfair competition of the most exasperating kind.

State of the Law: Noncompetition

The precedents are hard to align into a body of black-letter rules because the states have adopted quite different approaches to the issues involved, either through the common law of unfair competition and trade-secret protection as interpreted by judges and/or because legislation has been enacted. The rights of the two contesting parties—employer and former employee—will often depend on where the action is brought and which state law the court elects to apply. Without attempting to review the authorities, certain general propositions can be extracted, with the caveat that they are just that—general in nature and subject to local exceptions.

First, an obvious point: if the employer, the boss, breaches the employment contract, the employee is released from at least his noncompetition and probably his nondisclosure promises. (In a given context, the obligation to respect trade secrets may exist independent of contract.) The situation dealt with in this section is termination of the relationship because the *employee* quits, either in breach of his agreement or because the agreement no longer requires him to stay on.

Secondly, if a postemployment constraint is connected with the sale of a business, courts are more likely to enforce a noncompetition provision. Assume Smith, the sole owner of Widget, Inc., sells all his stock to Jones. Smith agrees to stay on for a period as a consultant and, for two years thereafter, to stay out of the widget business. If Smith attempts to violate his promise, a court will justify intervention by construing the restraint as protection for the goodwill that Jones has just bought. In this instance, the noncompetition covenant need not be tied to the unfair use of information. The investor has bargained for certain assets from the issuer, including the issuer's promise to stay out of the business. (It is not clear why investors purchasing a partial interest in Smith's company are entitled to any less consideration if Smith elects to quit. The goodwill is dissipated in either event.)

Allied to the "sale of the business" concept is the notion that, if the noncompetition restraint is created in connection with the resale of a significant equity position back to the company, the liveliness of the restraint is enhanced. As a planning point, therefore, it makes sense from the issuer's vantage point to tie the restraint to a buy/sell arrangement respecting the employee's equity. (If the repurchase is at a penalty price—e.g., the employee's cost—or for a *de minimis* amount of stock, common sense would suggest that the stock transaction should lend little help to the restraint's validity.) The two provisions should be expressly tied together, maybe even contained in the same numbered paragraph. The linkage device is not, of course, foolproof. As is the case generally in this area, courts in various states and at various stages approach the issues variously. Some will invent ways to ignore the equity side of the transactions and invalidate the restraint, reasoning that, for example, the price does not reflect a sale of goodwill.

The repurchase-of-equity provisions create a further opportunity for the firm to escape the negative implications of a "covenant not to compete." If the employer is located in a state hostile to postemployment restraints, one possibility is to string out certain benefits for the employee—for example, payment for the stock or deferred salary—and then provide for forfeiture if the employee winds up working for a competitor.

Alternatively, the former employer can sue the *new employer*, not the employee, for tortious interference, coupled with an allegation of wrongful misappropriation of proprietary information; the remedy sought in such a case is damages, but the object of the exercise is equitable in nature, to intimidate the competitor and/or the potential investors so that they refrain from infringing on the former employer's domain. To repeat a prior point, the plaintiff's claim is that noncompetition restraints are generally justified as necessary to enforce in the real world the underlying obligation not to misappropriate the employer's rights to its proprietary information. The idea is that once the employee has been allowed to join a rival firm, the damage has been done, the horse is out of the barn.

The gloss of "reasonableness" colors the discussion and holdings, meaning that the judges are consulting what they perceive to be the equities and common sense of the situation. Thus, the longer the employee has been employed and/or the higher his station in the company, the more likely a restraint will be enforced. A narrowly focused restraint will be more successful than one which bars the employee from working in "any competitive job anywhere in the world." The more sensitive the data to which the employee is privy, the likelier an injunction becomes. Indeed, injunctive relief is possible even in the absence of a contract if the secrets are particularly critical, but the failure of the employer to insist on a contract can be highly dangerous; the employer's lassitude cheapens its later assertions that the information is vital, and may, in fact, constitute a lack of vigilance which negates the employer's rights under the law of trade secrets.

chapter twelve

How to Go to the Promised Land (i.e., Go Public)

The initial public offering, routinely abbreviated as the IPO, is a familiar financing device; almost every public company has had an IPO. However, the maturity of companies offering securities to the public for the first time started to shrink in the late 1960s as new and unseasoned issuers tested the waters. A new breed of underwriters—Charles Plohn was the 1960s' paradigm—grew up to produce for public consumption shares in early-stage companies, on occasion before the issuers had seen their first quarter of black ink. Public finance became a viable option for companies that needed cash to stay in business. "Go bankrupt or go public?" was the jocular question founders would ask themselves in that rising, rambunctious market. IPO in this sense means more than the first public offering. In the venture-capital context, it means the culmination of the "exit" plan, the date on which the shares held by the founder, employees, and investors will become liquid and their plan to cash in their chips will approach fruition.

While many of the 1960s' underwriters (and more of their clients) are no longer in existence, the phenomenon persists. As one might expect, fast-rising markets are fertile ground for IPOs. The volume lessens, but not to zero, in down markets; many of the underwriters which grew up to service the IPO market have not only survived but flourished—Hambrecht & Quist is a prominent example. Moreover, access to the process for first-time issuers was simplified: first, with the adoption in 1979 of the Form S-18, available for offerings by non-public issuers not in excess of $7.5 million; and, quite recently, by the Small Business Initiative, which, for firms with less than $25 million in revenues, substitutes Form SB-2 for S-18 (in the process discarding the $7.5-million cap) and ameliorates post-IPO periodic reporting requirements by substituting Regulation SB-standards for the more rigorous requirements of Regulations S-K and S-X. Hence, the IPO option is in front of almost all early-stage companies—not the best option in every case, but one that requires consideration.

WHETHER OR NOT TO "GO PUBLIC"

There are two major issues facing a start-up considering an IPO: how to do it most effectively, and, secondly, whether to do it at all. The second is the threshold question. Will the issuer be able to raise capital cheaply and more efficiently on the wings of an IPO than with any other method, taking into account the long-range consequences of becoming a public company?

On the plus side, the culture of venture capital is heavily involved with the proposition that the terms "public company" and "rich entrepreneur" are synonymous. Indeed, the home-run payoffs for celebrated founders are usually identified with a public stock sale. A public market entails (although not for everybody) liquid securities, a classic exit strategy for founders and other shareholders. Moreover, to the extent equity is being raised for corporate purposes, the price of capital obtainable from the public will usually be cheaper because any commodity that can be freely sold is intrinsically more valuable than its illiquid counterpart.

There are collateral benefits as well, beyond price and liquidity. Thus, the company's stock is often purchased by its customers and suppliers and their interest in the company's profits and products is stimulated. A public company can do a broad, national public-relations job; a well-prepared prospectus projects the company's image favorably from the start. A public market helps stockholders with their estate-tax problems, it allows them to diversify, and it simplifies appraisal problems. And, the company now has so-called Chinese Currency with which to make additional acquisitions, meaning shares selling at a high multiple of earnings and, therefore, preferable to cash when buying other companies. Finally, with exceptions imposed by state securities administrators and the stock exchanges, the regulatory issues in an IPO process entail only adequacy of disclosure; ostensibly, the SEC is not authorized to delve into the merits of the offering.

There are, however, significant minuses. For example, an IPO takes time: the issuer and underwriter need sixty to ninety days to get ready, and the period between filing with the SEC and the effective date takes at least another month or so. Many an issuer undergoes the time-consuming and expensive process, only to see the process abort at the last instant because the IPO "window" has closed; if the issuer has counted on the proceeds of an IPO, the result can be a disaster. Moreover, there are significant transaction costs. Underwriters can receive up to 15 percent (more or less) of the price of the offering; legal and accounting expenses can bring the total costs up to 25 percent of the money raised. Fees and expenses involved in private placements, on the other hand, are ordinarily well under 10 percent. Moreover, once the issuer is public, a number of new legal requirements attach to the conduct of its business. Thus, a public company has to file periodic reports with the SEC (quarterly and annually) plus flash reports when significant events occur. The thrust of these documents is financial, letting the auction markets know how the company is doing on a short-term basis, in itself a potential problem for a management which is unconvinced that the market's avarice for short-term results is sensible business strategy. The annual meeting becomes a major event—proxies are solicited with an expensive, printed information document complying with the SEC's proxy rules, the disclosure heavily oriented toward exposing management's compensation package in a manner that suggests key executive compensation is one of the principal clues for analysts to unravel in judging corporate performance (a curiously puritanical view since private analysts' reports seldom mention top-management compensation as a principal benchmark of a firm's prospects). Beyond the required reports, the public company must give daily consideration to current disclosure of important events. As yet, the courts have not required instant press releases; absent insider trading, issuers are not, explicitly at least, required to go beyond compliance with the SEC's periodic (monthly on certain issues, otherwise quarterly and annually) disclosure rules, but that position is eroding. Thus, the New York Stock Exchange lectures issuers on the desirability of instant news and special exceptions to the general rule threaten the company's ability to remain silent (e.g., a duty to correct false rumors). Further, a public company is exposed to "strike suits," litigation initiated by underemployed lawyers ostensibly on behalf of a shareholder (usually with an insignificant stake), but in fact designed to corral legal fees. The courts countenance such claims because they are thought to have therapeutic value, restraining management excesses in an era when the public shareholders are otherwise disenfranchised. Finally, a public company can be taken over by a raider in a hostile tender. It is possible to insert so-called shark-repellent measures in the charter prior to the IPO—supermajority provisions, staggered boards, blank-check preferred stock—but the underwriters may balk.

Difficult rules also impact individuals associated with a public company: the directors, officers, and major shareholders. They are, for example, subject to a curious rule which recaptures any profit—called "short-swing" profit—they realize on sales and purchases of the company's stock matched within a six-month period. The statute becomes hard to follow at the margin, and its consequences are severe. Moreover, the threat that an insider will be deemed to have traded on "inside information" means that insiders can safely trade only during specified window periods, that is, immediately after the annual or quarterly reports come out; in a curious sense, insiders are not more liquid than they were before the IPO. Moreover, apart from requirements, the onset of a public venue can be embarrassing. The Antar family, when it sold one million common shares of Crazy Eddie, Inc. to the public, had to disclose that the family had been virtually using the company as a private bank. Spendthrift Farms, the breeding stable owned by the Combs family, has now been liquidated. When stock was sold to the public, a number of insider dealings between the family and the stable were revealed. Apparently those practices continued after the company became public, litigation ensued, and the result has been a more or less forced liquidation.

PREPARATION FOR THE PUBLIC OFFERING

The planning steps prior to a public offering are outlined in a number of source materials, emphasizing the increase in formality involved in the transition from a private to a public company. Some of the less obvious points which deserve mention have to do with corporate structure. The requirement that the financial statements be audited is well known. However, issuers on occasion forget that the recent acquisition of a significant, unaudited subsidiary may make it impossible to present the requisite audited financials when desired. Moreover, it is often necessary to recapitalize the enterprise. Cross-ownership arrangements must be eliminated and multiple affiliates consolidated so that the public buys an interest in all the eggs, contained in a single basket. Some IPO candidates, veterans of multiple financing rounds, have as many as eight series of preferred stock outstanding. If an IPO does not, by its terms, trigger conversion, negotiations are in order to clean up the balance sheet and make it understandable to prospective investors.

The Prospectus

The principal disclosure document in a public financing is the prospectus, that portion of the registration statement distributed to offerees and investors. The checklist for describing the company and the offering in the prospectus is Regulation S-K, directly applicable to Form S-1 Registration Statements. (Regulation S-B, a simplified version of S-K, governs the use by small business issuers of Form SB-2; for purposes of simplicity, it will be assumed in this discussion that S-K governs.)

The preparation of the prospectus is, in one sense, easy. The first cut at drafting entails selecting a comparable prospectus relating to a security already public marking it up, using the magic of optical scanning devices and word-processing equipment to take the drudgery out of the chore. Moreover, the preparation of the prospectus is governed by specific SEC advice—Regulation S-K (or Regulation S-B) and the instructions on the form used (S-1 or SB-2)—which give relatively precise directions as to the topics to be covered in the document, and, on occasion, how to cover them; for example: "Describe the general development of the business during the past five years. Describe the business done and intended to be done by the registrant and its subsidiaries, focusing upon the registrant's dominant industry segment." The road map for prospectus drafting is well defined; even a first-time draftsman should have little concern that something has been totally overlooked if he studies the precedents carefully.

To do the job properly, however, it is useful to ponder what it is the SEC is trying to accomplish. Thus, the intended thrust of Regulation S-K is to reduce the amount of boilerplate which might creep into documentation—to make the prospectus informative. For some time, the Commission has been criticized by commentators (including a perennial scold named Homer Kripke) for the fact that disclosure in unregistered placements is ordinarily more meaningful than the ritualistic language in statutory prospectuses, thereby standing the whole thrust of securities regulation on its head and opening the regulators up to their most feared criticism—irrelevance; the markets would function better without them. Tired of rainy weather, the SEC legislated sunshine in Regulation S-K and the instructions to forms S-1 and SB-2, attempting to reduce formalistic disclosure and put meat on the bones of the statements made. For example, the regulation now requires a section titled, "Management's Discussion and Analysis of Financial Condition and Results of Operations" (MD&A), in which the SEC tries to hold management's feet to the fire, requiring the type of candor one would expect in a question-and-answer session between the issuer's chief financial officer and security analysts. The regulation calls for mention of such matters as "trends . . . that are reasonably likely to result in the registrant's liquidity increasing or decreasing in any material way . . . [and] unusual or infrequent events . . . that materially affected reported income."

In considering how to phrase the language, one should also keep in mind a canon from which the SEC has never retreated: that public-disclosure documents should be decipherable by a nonexpert, a layman. It is true, as critics point out, that more than 75 percent of the action in the public markets is the result of professionals trading with professionals. Moreover, the Commission has undergone a major reorientation in its attitude toward disclosure by mature public companies, allowing issuers which report periodically to the public to cannibalize those reports for purposes of assembling a registration statement covering newly issued securities. Nonetheless, where new entrants to the public markets are concerned, the SEC has not accepted the thesis that a document which gives up its secrets to sophisticated analysts constitutes adequate disclosure. The prospectus must be drafted with that attitude in mind—coherent information assembled coherently, not only an informative but a "readable" document. Indeed, as a climax to its repeated attempts to render the availability of filed disclosure documents more user-friendly, on October 1, 1998 the SEC's "plain English" rules became effective for all registration statements filed after that date. (The rules do not cover reports on Forms 10K, 10Q, or 8K, or Proxy Statements filed under the '34 Act.) The rules are quite bland: use the active voice, avoid long sentences, avoid jargon and multiple negatives, and so forth. To help drafters of prospectuses, the SEC has published *A Plain English Handbook*, an unremarkable compendium designed to persuade people to turn to the principles announced in *The Elements of Style* by Strunk and White and/or the *Oxford English Dictionary*.

The principal concern of the securities bar has been that the rules increase the threat of liability, including allegations by plaintiff's lawyers based on violations of the rules themselves. It remains to be seen whether this spectre will eventuate.

The real problem, of course, is that preparation of the prospectus has become even more time consuming and expensive, despite the Commission's attempts at reform. A volatile market, back-up at the

SEC staff level extending the comment period, and other factors (including increased severity by the SEC on accounting issues so as to create "transparency") is making the initial public offering process more perilous and expensive than it has been in the past.

While prospectus writing is an art which does not require years of expertise to master (the plethora of prior examples allowing one to plagiarize shamelessly from the work product of others), that is not to say that experience is immaterial. The behind-the-scenes by-play centers around anticipating the comments likely to be made by the SEC staff (assuming, as is likely to be the case with an IPO, the prospectus is subject to "full review"), thereby shortening the length of the "letter of comment" and, more importantly, the comment period. Counsel's primary obligation in preparing an IPO (after making sure the presentation is accurate) is to get the registration statement effective as quickly as possible; market "windows" for IPOs come along every now and then and it is up to the participants to get the issue out on the street before the window closes. Thus, if the first draft of the prospectus asserts, without more, that the issuer is the "leading manufacturer" of widgets in the country, the SEC staff will routinely respond, "prove it." If the "Use of Proceeds" section is composed of routine language (i.e., "working capital"), the staff will try to extort greater specificity. Unfortunately, the staff does not publish its letters of comment. Some source materials have, however, reproduced sample letters and a survey of those materials will give a sense of the staff's favorites.

Some information the staff may zero in on can be confidential—the selling price of the issuer's products to major customers, for example—and the issuer will attempt to persuade the staff that such is not necessary for a complete presentation. Formally requesting confidential treatment is open to the registrant, but that course of action still leaves sensitive information in a government file, where Freedom of Information requests may uncover it; hence, informal persuasion is the preferred course. No amount of persuasion, however, is likely to eliminate certain sensitive disclosures mandated by Regulation S-K (e.g., the name of any customer representing 10 percent or more of the issuer's business).

No matter how carefully the prospectus is prepared, an IPO must await the letter of comment, and, other than nagging telephone calls, there is nothing the issuer can do but wait for it. Once a registration statement has been filed, within a couple of days (not more than four) a staff member will advise whether or not it will be reviewed. Registration statements not to be reviewed can be effective in as short a period as forty-eight hours; IPOs are routinely subjected to review and a first-time registrant can expect a 25- to 30-day period before receiving staff comments. Once the letter is received and responded to, then the procedure is to ask (two days in advance) for effectiveness at a particular date and time, a practice known for technical reasons as a "request for acceleration." Acceleration is conditioned on a widespread circulation of the preliminary, or red-herring prospectus (so called because there is a legend in red on the preliminary prospectus) among the selling group. Under Rule 430A, it will no longer be necessary to file the amendment filling in the price of the security, the underwriting syndicate, underwriting discounts, etc., and awaiting Commission clearance; the registration statement may now be declared effective, and the price (and discounts and syndicate members) filled in within five days.

LIABILITY

Disclosure in an IPO is inextricably bound up with the issue of liability. Who, and under what circumstances, repays the investors if there has been a material misstatement or omission which impacts the postoffering price of the stock? The issuer is, for all practical purposes, absolutely liable under §11 of the '33 Act, but the issuer may be unable to respond. The directors, as signers of the registration statement, have a heavy burden, which stretches to all those who, under §12, may be considered "participants" in the sale (i.e., insiders and promoters who participate in the transaction). In fact, counsel may be liable if intimately involved in the preparation of the materials; even major shareholders can be caught.

Moreover, underwriters are expressly liable, subject to a so-called due-diligence defense, under §11, and experts (e.g., lawyers and accountants) are liable for errors in the "expertised" portions, meaning the legal opinions and certified financial statements. The issues are complicated by the fact that, in dealing with liability, plaintiffs have access to a multiplicity of liability-creating provisions: for example, Sections 11, 12(2) and 17(a) of the '33 Act and §10b and Rule 10b(5) under the '34 Act. The threat of liability bites, of course, most sharply in an initial public offering, when all the information about the issuer is being presented for the first time.

Due Diligence

Choking off liability if the stock price plunges after the effective date requires counsel and the underwriters to execute a defensive game plan, designed to convince a judge and jury that they had vetted the required disclosures with the requisite care. This due-diligence defense to an action, based on §11 and available to all but the issuer, depends on the defendant establishing he had reasonable ground to believe the registration statement was accurate after "reasonable investigation," the latter phrase having been equated in common parlance with the exercise of due diligence. There is no one source which will outline to the issuer and the underwriters how far the diligence of their management and advisers should proceed. Some law firms prefer to work from a checklist; indeed, the NASD once composed a 16-item list as a minimum standard, but it was never adopted. A contrary view is held by those who believe that a checklist is a Christmas present to the plaintiff's lawyer, affording him an opportunity to inquire why certain items have been omitted. The widely cited *BarChris* decision is a learned opinion by a former partner of a prestigious Wall Street firm who set up standards which even the most diligent counsel would find hard to meet.

In the abstract, of course, elegant due diligence is a "motherhood" issue. Thus, one commentator suggests "counsel should consider making checks on the reputation and experience of its officers, including ordering Dun and Bradstreet and Proudfoots' reports. . . . The Company's directors should be investigated as well as the management." Practitioners in the field, however, may find academic procedures beyond the practical.

One relatively inexpensive way to limit exposure is to write an expansive and gloomy "risk-factors" or "special-factors" section. Regulation S-K requires a risk-factors recitation "if appropriate" and specifies that, if one is included, it should appear immediately following the cover page or summary. In a venture-backed IPO (as in a private placement), such a section is almost always "appropriate." Language calculated to avoid lawsuits is also appropriate in the so-called MD&A section, in which Regulation S-K requires "Management's Discussion of and Analysis of Financial Condition and Results of Operations." Since that discussion calls for disclosure of "trends," "forward-looking information . . . [such as] future increases in the cost of labor and materials" and oxymorons such as "known uncertainties," the opportunity is squarely faced for throwing in cautionary language likely to help contain subsequent litigation by identifying all the possible negative contingencies. The artist will play the two-handed game: "on the one hand, competition is increasing, while on the other we think our product stands out."

The distinction between a public and a private offering in terms of the potential liability for the promoters and participants continues to broaden. Misstatements or omissions in publicly distributed prospectuses are, in the opinion of most practitioners, an occasion for strict liability, regardless of whether the purchase of the securities in fact was misled by the statement or omission. The law has not yet seen the case which definitively alters the very heavy burdens Judge MacLean, in his *BarChris* opinion, laid on a defendant sued under §11 of the '33 Act, except with respect to so-called forward-looking statements; in that context, the courts have been more likely to exculpate the issuer if the paragraphs are surrounded with language which "bespeaks caution." Indeed, in private offerings generally, particularly private placements to sophisticated investors, the investors are bound by the terms of the document, including particularly the risk factors enumerated therein, whether they read the pamphlet or not. Moreover, while the issue is beyond the scope of this text, the courts have been eating away at the underpinnings of plaintiffs' actions based on Rule l0b-5 of the '34 Act. Rule l0b-5 is the avenue by which plaintiffs traditionally have traveled into federal court based on alleged misconduct in the private purchase or sale of securities. In recent years, that avenue has been narrowed by the imposition of a scienter standard; the stiffening of privity requirements; the shortening of the statute of limitations; and, finally, by cutting off the plaintiffs' access to alders and abettors, the deep-pocketed law and accounting firms who participate as advisers in the placement.

"DIRECTED SHARES" AND "HOT ISSUES"

The NASD also supervises how stock in an IPO is allocated, a requirement that overlaps with the SEC's rules against manipulative practices. Thus, the interpretation with respect to "free-riding and withholding" limits the practice of "free riding," that is, allocating "hot" stock (stock in an issue which immediately goes to a premium) as a disguised extra benefit to the underwriter and its special friends. A pattern of the same customers consistently participating in private placements immediately prior to a given underwriter's public offerings will be closely scrutinized. Moreover, the NASD imposes a standard of reasonableness on the amount of stock the issuer reserves for its friends: "issuer-directed securities." Obviously, upon an IPO, it is good business to reserve stock for customers and others who can help the firm in the future. Since the NASD is interested, however, in bona fide public offerings, it insists that the amount of issuer-directed securities bear a "reasonable relationship" (interpreted by one commentator as 10 percent) to the total amount offered and the favored purchasers be "directly related to the conduct of the issuer's business." The ban on allocating stock to restricted persons because of their NASD-member affiliation has posed problems for issuers who would also sell stock to venture funds and other investment pools which might have an attenuated affiliation which taints the fund—a limited partner of a limited partner in the fund in question is an NASD affiliate. The NASD has submitted proposals to relieve this conundrum to its members for approval.

A special section of the Rule, entitled "Venture Capital Restrictions," applies exclusively to IPOs and locks up for ninety days all stock (not just cheap stock) owned by the underwriter unless the offering price was established by an independent co-manager which does not own stock (or the question is *de minimis*). The NASD approval process for a new issue is currently about five to six weeks. The letters of comment fall under four categories: "defer review" means that there is not enough information even to begin review; "defer opinion" means initial information is required on a limited number of pending issues; a "no objection" letter indicates that compensation is reasonable; and an "unreasonable letter" means that disciplinary proceedings will be instituted if the offering proceeds.

LOCK UPS AND OTHER OBSTACLES TO LIQUIDITY

The final act in the IPO drama has to do with stock that is not offered in the initial floatation, but held by the insiders and not scheduled to be sold into the public markets until after the registration statement has become effective. Stock that does not flow through the public offering process is, in the jargon of the trade, "restricted," meaning that it has never been registered but it is nonetheless eligible for sale by the holders subject to certain constraints, the first of which is a contractual constraint imposed generally on the company and its underwriters and called the "lock up." A lock up, as discussed earlier, means that, for a period of time (usually 180 days) following the effective date of the IPO, major insiders of the company (the founders, the angel investors, key employees who obtain stock either directly or through the exercise of options, and the VCs), are committed by contract to withhold any shares from the market. The idea is that selling pressure from insiders could depress prices and create an overhang that would inhibit potential buyers of the stock offered in the IPO from purchasing shares.

Rule 144

The second constraint is created by rule, and specifically Rule 144. Since this rule comes into play whenever restricted stock is being sold into the public markets, a discussion in some detail is called for.

Rule 144 was published by the SEC in 1972 to clarify the rules governing the ability of a holder of restricted securities to resell his shares to the public. The problem is as old as the unhappy draftsmanship that went into the original Securities Act of 1933. That statute appears to provide that every sale of stock must be registered under the '33 Act, an absurd proposition; the New York Stock Exchange, where transactions take place in microseconds, would close down. Section 4(l) of the '33 Act comes to the rescue by exempting transactions by persons other than the "issuer" (primary transactions) or an "underwriter." This appears simple enough; all secondary (i.e., nonissuer) transactions are exempt. The drafters, however, elected to put the substance of the rule in the definition of the term "underwriter." That term includes the types of entities and people common sense would denote as underwriters—the members of the investment-banking syndicate underwriting the placement—plus two additional types, called "statutory" underwriters, namely: (1) persons who purchased their stock from an issuer "with a view to . . . the distribution of any security," and (2) persons "directly or indirectly controlling" the issuer. (The term "distribution" means public distribution.) Using this language, the SEC spread its jurisdiction over secondary transactions in two principal situations: the stock sold had never been registered under the '33 Act (so-called investment-letter or restricted stock), and/or the seller controlled the issuer (so-called control stock). As the SEC reads the §4(l) and the definition of "underwriter," all secondary transactions should *not* be exempt, rather only those involving trades of stock *other than* "letter" stock or control stock.

The fear, of course, was that the registration and disclosure provisions of the '33 Act could otherwise be eroded. If all secondary transactions were exempt, a nonregistered public offering could occur whenever the issuer could find someone to buy the stock, hold it for a little while, and then "decide" to sell it publicly; or the owner of a controlling interest in the firm could start to sell off his position, acting as the "alter ego" of the issuer.

To close what it perceived as loopholes, the staff took a long view of the phrase, "with a view to." If Start-up, Inc. sells stock in an exempt private transaction to Smith (under, say, §4(2) of the '33 Act), Smith resells in a private transaction to Brown, and Brown wants to sell to the public, the sale by Brown is nonexempt because Smith and Brown, *taken collectively*, purchased from the issuer "with a view to" a distribution. This notion involves a tortured reading of the language of the Act (by way of contrast, the definition of "restricted securities" in Rule 144 expressly uses the terms "directly or indirectly from the issuer . . . in a transaction *or chain of* transactions") but was an obvious follow-up step if the SEC did not want unregistered offerings escaping the net.

The awkwardness of the drafting did not, in the final analysis, chill the secondary market. The SEC and the courts worked the language around until it made some modicum of sense. While the statutory language related the registration requirements to the nature of the *transaction*, the real initial inquiry focused on what *kind* of stock the holder was trying to sell—was it letter stock because it had never been registered, and/or was it control stock because of who the holder was—a controlling person? If the stock one held was tainted, then the question was not so much *whether* but *when* the stock could be sold under §4(l) of the '33 Act as a nonevasive secondary sale without the necessity either of imposing investment-letter restrictions on the new buyer (maintaining illiquidity and thereby lowering the price), or registering the stock publicly (thereby incurring expense). It was obvious that at some point the regulators should be able to relax, to allow a secondary sale to progress under §4(l) regardless of the control status of the holder or the unregistered status of the stock, because the fear of evasion had abated with the passage of time. And that question was frequently addressed, albeit in some of the unhappiest stories in securities regulation. On occasion, the securities bar actually had to work with subjective tests—what was the "intent" (the "view") of Smith when he bought his shares from Start-up, Inc.? Did he truly "intend" to hold for "investment purposes"? If he later said he was changing his mind, did he do so just because he didn't like the stock anymore or because of a valid "change of circumstances," perhaps the loss of his job or a dreaded disease? Nonsense piled upon nonsense as counsel struggled with a series of no-action letters issued by the SEC staff, reading the tea leaves to figure out when their clients could sell without registration and without continuing the investment-letter restrictions.

Finally, the so-called Wheat Report (an SEC report from a blue-ribbon commission headed by Frank Wheat) engendered Commission action, leading to the promulgation in 1972 of Rule 144, a rule which allows the holders of control or letter stock to sell their shares publicly (no registration and no investment letters) in accordance with the provision of the Rule. The problem of letter stock is now more or less at rest, the qualifier required by the fact that staff interpretations now number more than one thousand and deal with exotic situations the Rule does not decide explicitly.

Rule 144 has one important threshold: it is not a back-handed opening through which shareholders can drive an unregistered IPO. Thus, Rule 144 generally applies only to stock in a company that is already publicly held. (That does not necessarily mean that the securities of the issuer have been registered and sold under §5 of the '33 Act; a company can—indeed must—become public over time if and as the number of shareholders exceeds five hundred.) The emphasis in the Wheat Report is on dissemination of information periodically and currently, shying away from the big-bang theory, which placed so much stock in the contents of a public registration statement. If the information is out in the marketplace, Rule 144 suggests, investors can trade. Indeed, a company with fewer than five hundred shareholders may voluntarily supply the requisite information so as to bring Rule 144 into play, but the absence of any public float makes it unlikely many would go that route (and Rule 144 is not available to issuers). If the information must be assembled and published to accommodate a secondary seller, why not create a real public offering with an IPO?

For the control person, the "manner" and "volume-of-sale" limitations are never lifted as long as the control relationship continues to exist (and for three months thereafter). For the holder of unregistered shares (control or no control), no sales may be made publicly for one year. During the second year, both controlling and noncontrolling persons can sell subject to "volume" and "manner-of-sale" restrictions, sales which are referred to as "dribbling out" the stock. After two years, noncontrolling persons can sell unregistered stock more or less as they choose. This table indicates the impact of the Rule:

Unregistered Stock

Holding Period	1 Year	1–2 Years	After 2 Years
Control	no sales	dribble out	dribble out
Noncontrol	no sales	dribble out	free sales

Registered Stock

Control	dribble out	
Noncontrol	Not subject to the Rule at all	

In connection with the promulgation of Rule 144A, the SEC liberalized Rule 144 by providing that the holding period during which restricted securities remain restricted is to be calculated by starting the clock ticking when the securities are first issued. Previously, the relevant holding period—two or three years depending on the method of distribution and whether or not the seller was an "affiliate" of the issuer—was calculated by measuring the length of time the securities concerned had rested in the seller's portfolio. If, for example, three sellers each held the stock for eighteen months, the two-year holding period had not been satisfied. In an important concession, the holding period in the example cited would have been satisfied while the securities rested in the portfolio of the second seller, assuming that none of the holder/sellers were affiliates of the issuer. This is a significant improvement over the prior state of the law and simplifies substantially the diligence burden. Once (1) the date the securities were issued and (2) the fact that no one in the chain of title was an affiliate of the issuer have been established, then the holding period is both simple to calculate and easy (or at least easier) to satisfy. In the never-ending stand against evasion, however, the SEC draftsmen have grafted on a series of complementary rules which enlarge the holding period—lengthen it—if a case can be made that the hopeful seller did not truly "own" the securities in the sense he was entirely at risk. The holder cannot count the period during which his position was hedged by a companion short sale, for example. Conversely, stock acquired pursuant to a stock dividend has a holding period which starts when the underlying stock was acquired. For present purposes, one of the most critical of the supplementary rules provides that stock acquired pursuant to a stock option does not start to acquire longevity until the option is exercised, but the holding period for stock received upon the conversion of convertible stock is "tacked" back to the ownership of the original security. This can pose a significant problem in the case of nonqualified employee options, which are generally optimized if the holder can exercise and sell simultaneously.

chapter thirteen

Financing with Strategic Investors: Joint Ventures

No topic is currently hotter in corporate finance than joint ventures. However, there is some question whether there exists any profound and distinct body of learning, at least in the legal sense, that fits under the heading of joint ventures, or its euphemistic variations, "corporate partnering" or "strategic alliances." Thus, when and if Company *A* enters into research, production, and marketing arrangements with a partner, the question remains: "What, if anything, distinguishes a strategic partnership from an everyday distribution or joint marketing arrangement between participants at different levels in a product distribution chain?"

The seminars and source materials do not readily provide a response to the question. The discussions generally have to do with issues involving investment relationships and licensing agreements. Perhaps the best way to reflect on the nature of the beast is to note that the law tends to attach consequences to the *status* of parties. If *X* is a *citizen* of the United States versus, say, a *resident*, various results flow from that categorization. Similarly, if *Y* is a corporation, the law tells us what rights, powers, privileges, and immunities emanate from that fact. Curiously, however, our legal rule makers have not focused much attention on the formal elements of a "joint venture," or, more properly, that bundle of often dissimilar legal relationships which are colloquially grouped under the heading "joint venture." Thus, the form "joint venture" can describe almost any consensual commercial relationship between two parties, focused on a specific business purpose.

With that caveat, a few preliminary general observations are in order. Thus, again generally, joint ventures are entered into for profit, although one or more of the players may be not-for-profit entities. Again generally, a joint venture addresses a specific project—to promote a particular product, to commercialize a given area of research, to join hands across an international border—and that description implies limitations in scope and time. But some joint ventures are designed to be perpetual. English law treats joint ventures as special partnerships and that may be as good a definition as any.

If the venture is incorporated, a so-called corporate joint venture in which Venturers *A* and *B* are the shareholders, then the legal status of the venture is governed by the general corporation law of the state of incorporation. (A caveat: a minority of decisions suggests that the shareholders in corporate joint ventures may, for some purposes, be deemed partners.)

If the vehicle is not incorporated, it is likely the venture will be treated as a partnership, governed by the rules set out in the applicable state version of the Uniform Partnership Act. Note that a corporation does not exist unless it has been intentionally (and formally) organized as such. On the other hand, partnership will come into being if the parties behave like partners, whether or not they consciously will themselves to enter into a partnership relationship—indeed, even if they expressly deny they are partners. There are several important consequences resulting from partnership status, discussed *seriatim*.

Typical Business Contexts

While the possibilities are almost infinite, some of the more common include the following:

Disguised Sale

Typically, Venturer *A* will want to dispose of a low-basis, high-value asset. Instead of selling the asset outright to *B*, *A* and *B* will organize a joint venture (usually a partnership), exploit the asset jointly for a time, and then unscramble the omelette so that *A* gets the cash and *B* the asset. This technique, sometimes called a "mixing-bowl transaction" for obvious reasons, can be tax efficient but also involves tax risk if the parties are not exposed to significant operational risks during the venture's existence or the transaction, from soup to nuts, was agreed upon in advance. On the other hand, if the venturer interested in selling assets secures a credit-enhanced preferred return during the required operational period (say five years), then the sale in real economic terms may have occurred on Day 1, no tax having been incurred on the gain. The transaction may be particularly tasty from *X*'s point of view if *A* is able to borrow against its partnership interest as of the date the venture is organized. Again, however, the caveat: the IRS is not asleep, and a technique successful today may be attacked tomorrow; the IRS has ample weapons to rearrange transactions lacking sufficient business purpose. Thus, aggressively structured mixing-bowl transactions have been made more risky by the promulgation of a proposed regulation which would, on its face, allow the IRS to attack most any claims. Sponsors are now more conservative about skewing allocations of profits and losses attributable to contributed assets away from the contributing partner.

A Euphemism for a Licensing Agreement: An OEM Contract et al.

Any long-term contract—a license, a lease, OEM manufacture—can be called a joint venture if it suits the parties' interests. Thus, a high-tech start-up licensing software to, say, IBM may prefer to style the agreement as a "joint venture" since it lends cachet to the development-stage enterprise.

A Cross-Border Marketing and Distribution Arrangement

International joint venturers are increasingly popular. Venturer *A* makes a product in Detroit, the market is in Germany, but *A* has no real capacity, at any realistic level of cost, to market and distribute in Germany. The answer is a joint venture with a German firm (perhaps even a competitor) which understands the local market. The cross-border joint venture may also facilitate the permeation of trade barriers and avoid restrictions on foreign ownership of domestic industry, what one might call a "mercantilism-busting" joint venture.

R&D Joint Venture

The tax-driven R&D partnership, typically a partnership between a high-tech issuer and tax-averse investors, is no longer popular—a victim of the 1986 Tax Reform Act, plus the fact that many such partnerships turned out to be more trouble than they were worth. Early-stage companies need "big brother" financing, nonetheless. The current fashion, which has never been out of fashion, is a joint venture between a strategic investor and an early-stage issuer, sometimes intermediated by a co-investment from a venture-capital fund in which the strategic investor is a partner, the fund acting as a pathfinder for the strategic investor.

Risk-Sharing Joint Venture

On occasion, a project will be too large for any one firm to be able, or want, to undertake it. The ubiquitous joint ventures between oil companies to develop particular prospects exemplify this genre.

Pro-Competitive Joint Venture

If a given firm, number one in a given market, threatens to mop up its competitors by virtue of its overbearing market share, competitors down the ladder may joint venture, in lieu of merging, to preserve their existence in the market.

NEGOTIATION POINTS

Cultural Disconnect: An Alert

It is clear to the point of obviousness that there are cultural differences between the entrepreneurial mind-set and the corporate mentality, having largely to do not so much with perverse people but with the *structure* of large institutions. James Buchanan won the 1986 Nobel Prize in economics for elaborating elegantly on a more or less obvious proposition: that people within a political system behave so as to maximize their personal outcomes. Such is also the case in a large industrial organization, and it is critical that the founder understand the point so that he can appreciate what is motivating his corporate partners. He must understand that the corporation itself is an abstraction. It represents a basket of a number of interests, sometimes synchronized and sometimes competing. It acts, as only it can act, through people—a large number of people processing decisions vertically up and down the corporate hierarchy and horizontally from division to division. Theoretically, people in a large company are working together for the good of the institution; in fact, of course, they are often competitors. For some, their near-term, and perhaps long-term, interest is focused first on figuring out ways for each of them to succeed within the corporate structure, and, often as a complement to that strategy, figuring out ways that their competitors for desirable job opportunities fail; finally, often in distant third place, the players attempt to maximize the outcome of the corporation itself. This phenomenon was colorfully brought home to the author when his firm represented a major Midwestern corporation engaged, as a defendant, in product-liability litigation. The product in dispute had been initiated by manager *A*, who had since gone to other responsibilities within the corporation; direction to the litigation team was being provided by manager *B*. It became difficult to figure out the instructions being given by manager *B*; they seemed to be self-defeating, until the key to the Rosetta Stone made itself apparent: Manager *B* actually wanted his corporation to lose the lawsuit, thereby embarrassing manager *A* and maximizing manager *B*'s chances to beat *A* to the finish line—the job for which they were both competing. This lesson needs endless repetition when dealing with a major company. The people at the table have their own agendas, which do not necessarily coincide with the interests of the company for which they work.

Control

Control of a joint venture is usually vested in a committee composed of representatives of each side, the people most involved in the process and invested with the power of decision. As stated by E. Martin Gibson, then-president of the health and science group of Corning Glass: "The kiss of death for any joint venture is for its board to be a play board when the real power is back at corporate headquarters." When, as is often the case, the parties have discrete areas of responsibility—Start-up doing the research and Goliath providing the resources for sales, marketing, and distribution—Start-up's management may not realize how important it is that they have a voice in the management of Goliath's salesforce. If Start-up's management does not have a say in the decisions whether to discharge unproductive salespeople and replace them, to direct salespeople in the field to concentrate on high-profit lines of business, and to target particular customers, then its products can be at the mercy of distracted, uninterested salespeople concentrating on other items in Goliath's line and the venture can fail—an annoyance to Goliath but a disaster to Start-up. Funding provided by Goliath is ordinarily controlled by "milestones," achievement benchmarks which can be monitored by the controlling committee with respect to technical qualifications, on-time performance, and market penetration. Consultants are often employed to break ties if the parties disagree on progress payments against ambiguous milestones, an ambiguity that is often inherent because the "product," if truly the end result of experimentation, is shrouded in some mystery when the drafting occurs. The issue of cost overruns is often neglected in the initial drafting, usually to the detriment of Start-up, which must bargain for needed completion monies without a shred of leverage in the absence of contractual provisions.

As a practical matter, a system of reporting is critical to smooth sailing. Frequent reporting is needed to alert Goliath to a pending milestone and generally to maintain interest in the project among easily diverted managers in the Goliath organization.

Prenuptial Agreements

The failure to think through appropriate procedures for unwinding the venture is an often-encountered sin. Frequently, one of the venturers—the classic start-up—will have staked its business existence on the success of the venture. How can the *status-quo ante* be restored if the venture doesn't work, at least to the extent the start-up enjoys a residual chance at resuming independent existence? In drafting what amounts to a prenuptial agreement anticipating divorce, planners should focus on the questions set out below.

Rights of First Refusal, etc.

Further, many joint-venture agreements fail to cover the contingency that one of the venturers may want unilaterally to sell its interest, giving rise to controversy whether a right of first offer or first refusal should be implied. A more difficult issue is posed if the success of the joint venture is dependent on the continued operation of a segment of one of the venturers' main businesses. Reportedly, Sony was prepared to sue CBS to enjoin the sale of CBS's record division to anyone other than Sony, based on a long-standing joint-venture agreement between the two firms respecting, among other things, the manufacture of compact discs. If the venture is a general partnership, it is easier to imagine court-enforced restraints on the introduction of new proprietors called "partners" in view of the historical intimacy of the partnership relationship. This is no excuse, however, for failing to codify the parties' intention on this subject in a formal, comprehensive document—whether a partnership agreement or an agreement amongst shareholders. The touchiest area for negotiation, vide the CBS/Sony dispute, will be the responsibility of each venturer to maintain necessary infrastructure. If software company *A* joint ventures with hardware company *B* to exploit a particular system, should *B* be required to stay in the hardware business? What if *B* is losing money on that line? If *B*'s agreement is all-embracing, is the joint venture something *B*'s shareholders should vote on—what amounts to "hypothecation" or "lease" of substantially all *B*'s assets, perhaps?

Drag-Along Rights and Other Exit Levers

If the joint venture has a lengthy time horizon, one of the venturers may want to exit prematurely; perhaps it could use an earnings spike if unrealized appreciation were in fact to be realized. The unilateral sale of a venturer's individual interest is often inopportune, either because of contractual restrictions or economic realities. Accordingly, the drafting should (and often doesn't) cover a relatively lengthy menu of exit issues: registration rights (rarely employed as written), tag-along rights, compulsory liquidation, compulsory sale (herein called "drag-along" rights), and so forth.

Liquidation

Frequently, the assets of a joint venture are intangible: intellectual property, marketing "support," future services. In the event of liquidation, how is the ownership of such intangibles to be allocated? Assume the core asset is a trade secret, an item of property which can no longer be possessed exclusively (meaning it is no longer legal property) if it is no longer a secret: Can the noncontributing joint venturers be required to forget the secret? To discharge or reassign the employees who have become versed in it? To refrain from making or distributing products which are a direct or indirect consequence of the secret? If the assets of the venture are to be sold because the venturers can't agree, can a venturer be compelled to maximize the value of such assets (as in continuing to support software in the hands of the new owner) after the venture has been liquidated? "Ownership" is a complex concept, best analogized to a bundle of rights; the fact that "joint-venture law" is as yet unformed further complicates the problem. Joint tenancy in real-property law is outlined by well-developed concepts, but it would be a mistake to import the same to cover all possible joint ventures. As Walter Wheeler Cook once said, "The tendency to assume that a word which appears in two or more legal rules, and so in connection with more than one purpose, has and should have precisely the same scope in all of them runs all through legal discussions. It has all the tenacity of original sin and must constantly be guarded against."

The moral, of course, is (again) careful drafting.

THE DUTY OF CANDOR

What obligations does one joint venturer owe the others to disclose proprietary information which is related to the business of the joint venture but not part of its central core? This issue is part of a larger conflict-of-interest problem and includes (as discussed below) corporate opportunity and self-dealing. The fundamental question has to do, again, with the essential nature of joint ventures in general and the given joint venture in particular. Is the beast a partnership (implying duties of good faith and fair dealing which go beyond the four corners of the partnership agreement), or a limited-purpose vehicle? In the latter case, the argument is that the partners owe each other only those duties expressly set forth in writing. Hence, if venturer *A* possesses information which might be useful to the venture (and/or to *B*) but which *A* wishes at all costs to protect, *A* may remain silent. The opposing view derives from Judge Cardozo's language in a landmark case: "[j]oint adventurers, like copartners, owe to one another while the enterprise continues, the duty of the finest loyalty." The conflict problems are exacerbated if the joint venturers are otherwise competitors.

CORPORATE OPPORTUNITY AND SELF-DEALING

If *A* and *B*, both ethical drug companies, join hands to exploit a particularly expensive field of research, what happens if *A* independently uncovers a promising compound which might complement the joint venture's end products? Under the law of corporate opportunity as developed over the years, must *A* bring the development to the venture? Assume *A* does in fact offer the compound to the venture, can *A* charge any price it elects? Yet again, if the drafting is anemic, the court must marry its guesstimate as to the parties' original intent and reasonable expectations within the conceptual framework the court elects to apply to the animal it confronts—a partnership in Cardozo's sense, with the comprehensive fiduciary obligations Cardozo's prose suggests, versus a limited contractual relationship entailing no special duties other than those expressly written down.

Variations on this conflict theme are numerous. Thus, one venturer may wish to block the venture's expansion into a market the venturer assumes is its exclusive domain. The joint venture may generate commercially valuable information which one of the venturers may appropriate for use in its main line of business, perhaps to the detriment of another venturer's prospects. The difficulty in drafting responses to these contingencies is, of course, that there are so many of them.

Conclusion

As with any vibrant and energetic investment activity, the venture-capital norms and cultural artifacts are subject to rapid and frequent change; however, as with the game of baseball, there are certain verities which appear to be more or less eternal, or at least stoutly resistant to change.

The structure of a venture-capital fund, for example, today looks much like the first fund I worked on in 1963. The initial public offering process is fundamentally the same as it was when I spent my first night at the printer. The private-equity market is still inefficient, accounting in part for the enormous returns available on occasion to canny VCs.

On the other hand, there are a number of significant new developments: the rise of semiorganized angel investing is a positive phenomenon. And, the liberalization of the rules allowing pension and endowment funds to invest in early-stage enterprises has been an enormous boost. However, there remains a long list of improvements yet to happen, improvements in the rules, in the underlying structure, and in the culture which would liberate even more creative energy and create significant additional wealth, jobs, and technological advances.

The SEC's attempts, for example, to introduce productive efficiency into the private-capital markets have stalled since the enactment of Regulation D; there have been few, if any, subsequent examples of inspired rule making, with the possible exception of federal preemption of state securities regulation. Most of the Commission's initiatives have been false steps. We continue to have an unbridgeable chasm separating public companies from private companies. A sensible regulation would suggest, in my view, that there be comfort stations along the way, places in which adolescent firms could reside on their journey from the embryo to the IPO; ritualistic, hide-bound thinking has kept the regulators from even looking into the possibilities. Moreover, for all the SEC's efforts over the years, investors know a good deal less about small and microcap public companies (the great majority of which enjoy no analytical following whatsoever) versus the wealth of information (unearthed by due diligence with the benefit of projections) which professional private investors routinely access.

The short of the matter, however, is that, when viewing the landscape from, as they say, fifty thousand feet, our criticisms are, relatively speaking, quibbles. Venture capital is alive and well and its prospects are bright, riding as it is today a great technological revolution in the person of the Internet. The attempt in these pages has been to explain for the serious player how the game is in fact played: the rules, the customs, the norms, the financial technology, the myths (if you like), the conventional wisdom, everything equipping a participant to compete on a level playing field with the most experienced competitors.

.

index

about the author

JOSEPH W. BARTLETT is a partner at Morrison & Foerster, LLP in the firm's New York City office. He is also an adjunct professor at New York University School of Law. Mr. Bartlett is an expert in, among other things, corporate restructurings and venture-capital transactions. He has published numerous articles and books, including *Equity Finance: Venture Capital, Buyouts, Restructurings and Reorganizations; Corporate Restructurings: Reorganizations and Buyouts; Venture Capital: Law, Business Strategies and Investment Planning;* and *The Law Business: A Tired Monopoly.*

A former Undersecretary of Commerce, law clerk to Chief Justice Earl Warren, and President of the Boston Bar Association, Mr. Bartlett graduated from Stanford Law School, where he was president of the Law Review. He has been an acting professor of law at Stanford and an instructor in law at Boston University Law School. Mr. Bartlett has acted as counsel to and been a director of and shareholder in a number of development-stage companies during his 35-year career in the venture-capital business, and has been profiled in trade publications as one of the leading practitioners in venture capital nationwide.